NATIONAL GEOGRAPHIC
KiDS

AWESOME
Maths &
English
AGE 7-9

Get awesome at Maths and English!

Explore some of the world's most amazing animals and exercise brain cells on the way!

Four wild adventures open up fascinating facts about different creatures and provide practice for Maths and English:

- Marvel at **baby animals** while working through the **Maths** topics for **Ages 7–8**.

- Uncover **minibeasts and creepy crawlies** while stepping through the **Maths** topics for **Ages 8–9**.

- Size up some of the world's **smallest and largest animals** while stomping through the **English** topics for **Ages 7–8**.

- Admire **seashore creatures** while navigating the **English** topics for **Ages 8–9**.

Awesome adventures await... good luck, explorer!

Published by Collins
An imprint of HarperCollins*Publishers*
Westerhill Road
Bishopbriggs
Glasgow G64 2QT
In association with National Geographic Partners, LLC

NATIONAL GEOGRAPHIC and the Yellow Border Design are trademarks of the National Geographic Society, used under license.

First published 2020

ISBN 978-0-00-838881-2
10 9 8 7 6 5 4 3

A catalogue record for this book is available from the British Library

Printed in India by Multivista Global Pvt. Ltd.

If you would like to comment on any aspect of this book, please contact us at the above address or online.

natgeokidsbooks.co.uk
collins.reference@harpercollins.co.uk

Acknowledgements
P30, Jeff Rotman / Alamy.com;
P69, ©Paul Zahl /Science Photo Library
P72, ©Ger Bosma / Alamy.com
P78, 117 © Morley Read / Alamy.com
P84, 117 © Peter Chadwick/Science Photo Library
P85 © Alouise Lynch/Wikipedia
All other images are ©Shutterstock.com and ©HarperCollins*Publishers*
Authors: Pamela Wild, Alison Head and Melissa Blackwood
Publisher: Michelle I'Anson
Project Manager: Richard Toms
Cover Design: Sarah Duxbury
Inside Concept Design: Ian Wrigley
Page Layout: Ian Wrigley and Rose and Thorn Creative Services Ltd

Features of this book

Practice Tasks – activities to build confidence and improve skills

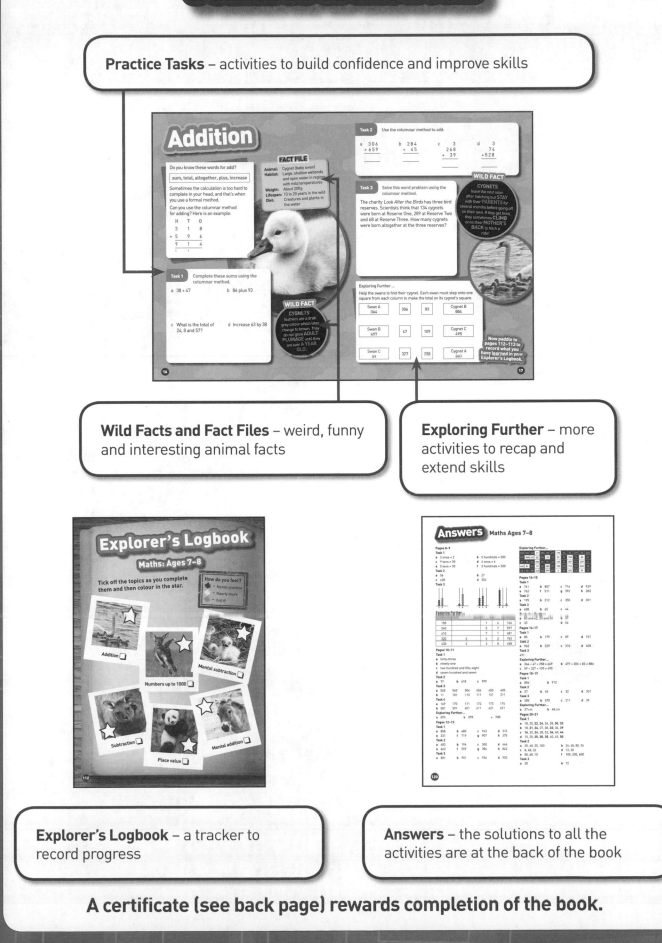

Wild Facts and Fact Files – weird, funny and interesting animal facts

Exploring Further – more activities to recap and extend skills

Explorer's Logbook – a tracker to record progress

Answers – the solutions to all the activities are at the back of the book

A certificate (see back page) rewards completion of the book.

Contents

Maths: Ages 8–9

English: Ages 7–8

English: Ages 8–9

Place value

A number can only be made up from the digits 1 2 3 4 5 6 7 8 9 and 0 (zero).

A digit's value (what it is worth) depends on which column it is placed in.

H T O

1	This 1 is in the ones column and is worth just 1
1 0	This 1 is in the tens column and is worth one set of 10
1 0 0	This 1 is in the hundreds column and is worth one set of 100

Zero is used as a place holder so that you know which column a digit is in when there are no column headings.

Task 1   Write down the value of the underlined digit.

a 49<u>2</u> _____

b <u>5</u>63 _____

c 2<u>9</u>0 _____

d 80<u>6</u> _____

e 3<u>5</u>9 _____

f <u>3</u>04 _____

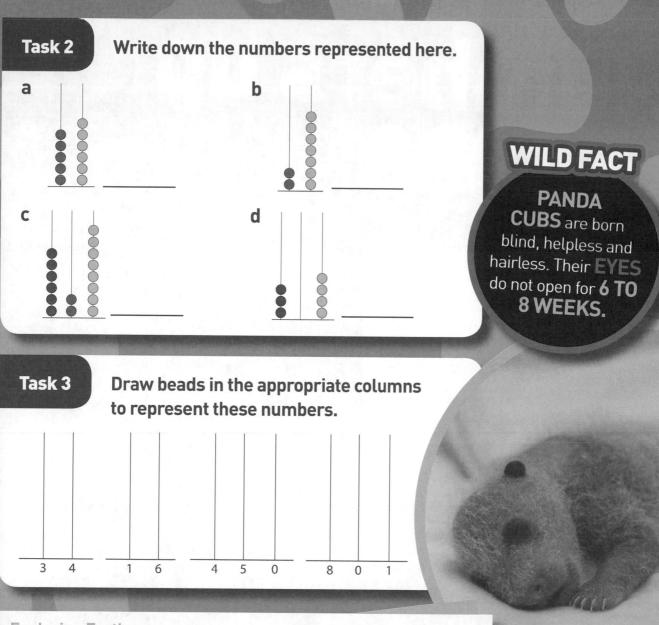

Task 2

Write down the numbers represented here.

a

b

c

d

Task 3

Draw beads in the appropriate columns to represent these numbers.

| 3 | 4 | | 1 | 6 | | 4 | 5 | 0 | | 8 | 0 | 1 |

Exploring Further ...

Help the cubs reach their mum. In the table below write down how many ones, tens and hundreds are needed to get from the first number to the last number. The first one has been done for you.

	First number	Hundreds	Tens	Ones	Last number	
	150		1	6	166	
	540				597	
	610				681	
	320				763	
	430				658	

Now turn to pages 112–113 to record what you have learned in your Explorer's Logbook.

Numbers up to 1000

Understanding the place value of numbers helps you to read, write, compare and order them.

Which number is bigger?

458   or   485

Discover how well you can do this and check whether you can count in ones, tens and hundreds.

FACT FILE

Animal: Fawn (baby deer)
Habitat: Woodlands, mountains and grasslands across Europe, Asia, North America and South America
Weight: Up to 6 kg at birth
Lifespan: Up to about 15 years
Diet: Mother's milk for first few weeks; at 6 weeks they start to eat vegetation

WILD FACT

A **FAWN** can stand about **HALF AN HOUR** after its birth. Within a few days, it can **OUTRUN** a human.

Task 1	Write these numbers in words.

a 43 _____

b 91 _____

c 258 _____

d 707 _____

Task 2 Write these numbers in figures.

a seventy-seven _____

b six hundred and eighteen _____

c nine hundred and ninety-nine _____

Task 3 Order these numbers from biggest to smallest.

a 405   540   450   504   545   454

_____

Order these numbers from smallest to biggest.

b 111   101   110   11   121   211

_____

Task 4 Fill in the gaps in the number sequences.

a 169   [   ]   171   172   [   ]   [   ]

b 581   591   [   ]   [   ]   [   ]   [   ]

Exploring Further ...

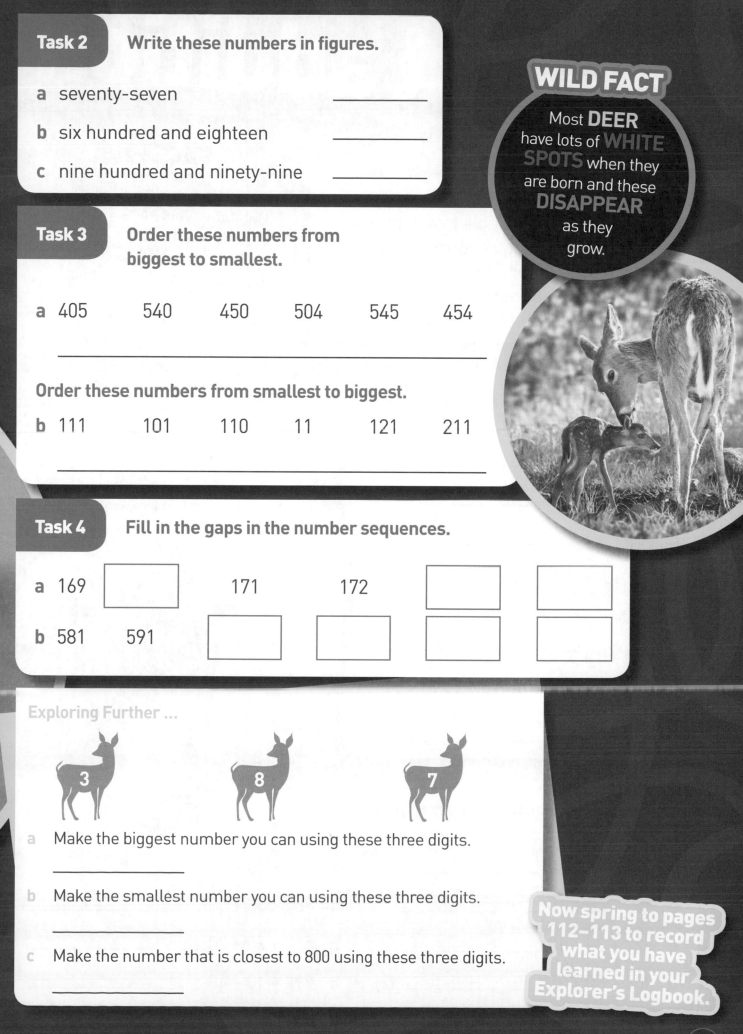

3   8   7

a   Make the biggest number you can using these three digits.

_____

b   Make the smallest number you can using these three digits.

_____

c   Make the number that is closest to 800 using these three digits.

_____

Now spring to pages 112–113 to record what you have learned in your Explorer's Logbook.

Mental addition

Good mental agility is key to being a good mathematician. Being able to **add in your head** accurately and quickly makes a huge difference to your confidence. So make sure you know your **number bonds** to 20 off by heart and practise them regularly.

Task 1 — Add these numbers in your head.

a 851 + 3 + 4 _____

b 673 + 5 + 2 _____

c 955 + 4 + 4 _____

d 307 + 4 + 2 _____

e 224 + 5 + 2 _____

f 713 + 3 + 3 _____

g 901 + 4 + 2 _____

h 364 + 5 + 1 _____

Task 2 — Add these numbers in your head.

a 432 + 20 + 30 _____

b 126 + 60 + 10 _____

c 250 + 40 + 10 _____

d 364 + 30 + 50 _____

e 622 + 30 + 10 _____

f 519 + 20 + 20 _____

g 304 + 50 + 30 _____

h 792 + 10 + 40 _____

Task 3

Now add these bigger numbers in your head.

a 481 + 400   _____

b 601 + 300   _____

c 236 + 600 + 100   _____

d 103 + 100 + 700   _____

WILD FACT

A **FOAL** can stand **ONE HOUR** after birth.

WILD FACT

WILD horses are usually **SHORTER** and have **ROUNDER** bellies than domestic horses.

Exploring Further ...

Find the name of Liz's foal. Colour the answer in the grid to each of the sums and the name will be revealed.

208	965	160	17	395	58	471	178	36	47	729	28	653
909	398	492	56	824	25	57	93	97	798	74	30	67
27	48	86	593	92	77	54	149	91	207	772	229	41
643	81	741	19	62	482	87	150	903	712	797	845	78
45	68	88	663	303	999	697	6	85	505	228	99	37

33 + 4 = ?	21 + 7 = ?	63 + 34 = ?	157 + 3 = ?	472 + 300 = ?
65 + 2 = ?	52 + 6 = ?	35 + 22 = ?	298 + 5 = ?	609 + 300 = ?
76 + 1 = ?	43 + 5 = ?	46 + 41 = ?	645 + 8 = ?	297 + 500 = ?
47 + 7 = ?	19 + 8 = ?	57 + 17 = ?	725 + 4 = ?	865 + 100 = ?
85 + 7 = ?	78 + 8 = ?	25 + 37 = ?	203 + 5 = ?	341 + 400 = ?
34 + 7 = ?	37 + 8 = ?	74 + 17 = ?	335 + 60 = ?	421 + 50 = ?
41 + 27 = ?	62 + 16 = ?	53 + 35 = ?	617 + 80 = ?	784 + 40 = ?
29 + 18 = ?	18 + 18 = ?	57 + 28 = ?	813 + 90 = ?	158 + 70 = ?

Now trot to pages 112–113 to record what you have learned in your Explorer's Logbook.

Mental subtraction

Subtracting in your head is a bit harder than adding.

You can take away the smaller number from the bigger one. For example:

68 – 5 = 63

```
        ← ─── – 5 ───
  |────────●────────────●──────|
 60       63           68     70
```

Alternatively, you can add from the smaller number to the bigger one to find the difference. For example:

74 – 46 = 28

```
        ─── + 28 ───────────→
  |────●────────────────●─────|
 40   46                74   80
```

Practise your number bonds! If you know that 8 + 9 = 17, then you also know that 17 – 8 = 9 and 17 – 9 = 8.

WILD FACT

EAGLE PARENTS are very **PROTECTIVE** of their chicks and one parent will usually **KEEP WATCH** over the nest.

FACT FILE

Animal: Eaglet (baby eagle)
Habitat: They often nest in tall trees or on high cliffs in Europe, Asia, Africa, North and South America, and Australia
Weight: About 4 kg at 6 weeks old
Lifespan: 20 to 30 years in the wild
Diet: Fed meat and fish from their mother

Task 1 — Subtract these numbers in your head.

a 764 – 3 _____

b 809 – 2 _____

c 722 – 8 _____

d 936 – 7 _____

e 792 – 30 _____

f 561 – 50 _____

g 482 – 90 _____

h 353 – 70 _____

Task 2 — Now subtract these bigger numbers in your head.

a 295 – 100 _____

b 612 – 300 _____

c 750 – 400 _____

d 901 – 600 _____

WILD FACT

It takes about **40 DAYS** for **EAGLE EGGS** to hatch.

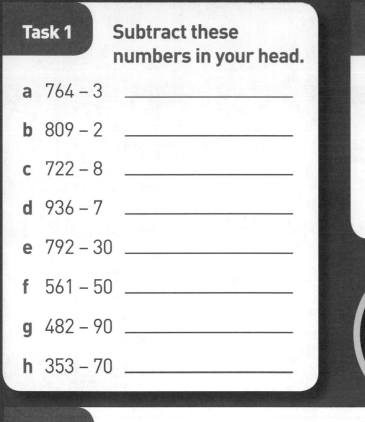

Task 3 — Solve these problems in your head.

a A scientist counted a total of 698 eagle eggs in a particular habitat. One week later, 90 of the eggs had hatched.

How many eggs were still to hatch? _____

b It took 108 days from when an eagle's egg was laid to the eaglet leaving the nest. If it took 43 days for the egg to hatch, how many days was the baby bird in the nest before it took its first flight? _____

c If 37 out of a total of 81 eagles in one part of Scotland are male, how many are female? _____

Exploring Further ...

83   29   37   33   62   54

a Which two pairs of numbers above have a difference of 21?

_____

b Which number is 17 less than 54? _____

c Which number is the answer to 62 minus 29? _____

d What is left when 29 is subtracted from 83? _____

Now fly to pages 112–113 to record what you have learned in your Explorer's Logbook.

Addition

Do you know these words for **add**?

sum, total, altogether, plus, increase

Sometimes the calculation is too hard to complete in your head, and that's when you use a formal method.

Can you use the columnar method for adding? Here is an example:

	H	T	O
	3	1	8
+	5	9	6
	9	1	4
	1	1	

FACT FILE

Animal: Cygnet (baby swan)
Habitat: Large, shallow wetlands and open water in regions with mild temperatures
Weight: About 200 g
Lifespan: 10 to 20 years in the wild
Diet: Creatures and plants in the water

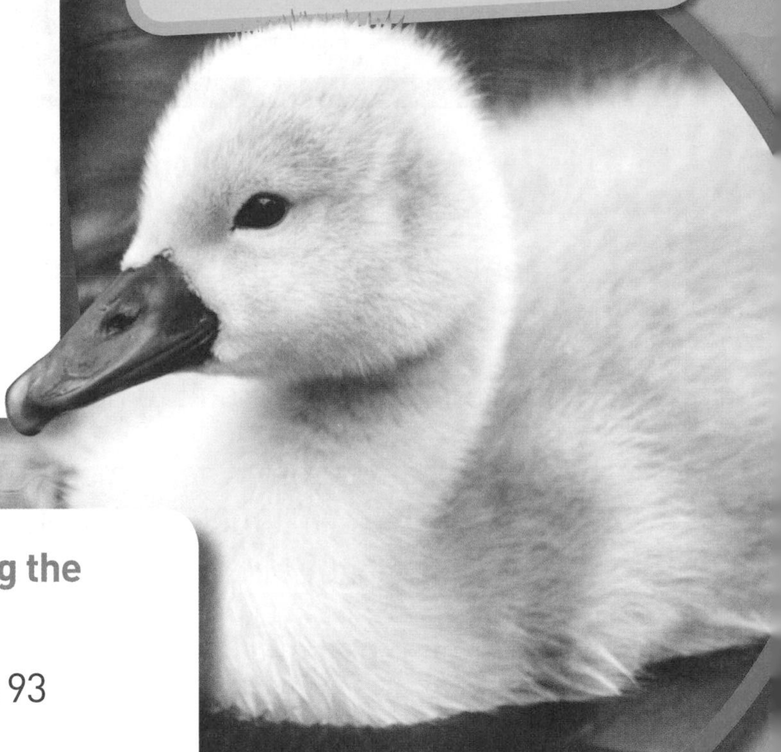

Task 1 **Complete these sums using the columnar method.**

a 38 + 47

b 86 plus 93

c What is the total of 24, 8 and 57?

d Increase 63 by 38

WILD FACT

CYGNETS' feathers are a drab grey colour which later change to brown. They do not grow **ADULT PLUMAGE** until they are over **A YEAR OLD.**

Task 2 Use the columnar method to add.

a   306
    + 659
    _____

b   284
    + 45
    _____

c   3
     268
    + 39
    _____

d   3
      74
    + 528
    _____

Task 3 Solve this word problem using the columnar method.

The charity *Look After the Birds* has three bird reserves. Scientists think that 134 cygnets were born at Reserve One, 289 at Reserve Two and 68 at Reserve Three. How many cygnets were born altogether at the three reserves?

WILD FACT

CYGNETS leave the nest soon after hatching but **STAY** with their **PARENTS** for several months before going off on their own. If they get tired, they sometimes **CLIMB** on to their **MOTHER'S BACK** to hitch a ride!

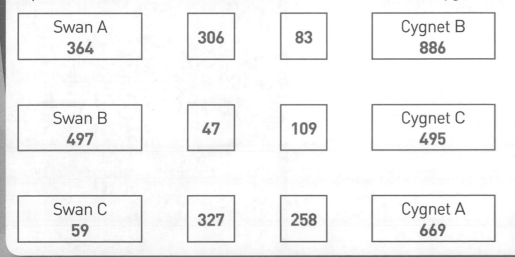

Exploring Further ...

Help the swans to find their cygnet. Each swan must step onto one square from each column to make the total shown with its cygnet.

Swan A 364	306	83	Cygnet B 886
Swan B 497	47	109	Cygnet C 495
Swan C 59	327	258	Cygnet A 669

Now paddle to pages 112–113 to record what you have learned in your Explorer's Logbook.

Subtraction

Subtraction is the opposite process to addition. For example:

$5 + 4 = 9$ Subtraction can undo this addition: $9 - 4 = 5$

$7 - 3 = 4$ Addition can undo this subtraction: $4 + 3 = 7$

Make sure you know the different words for subtraction: **take away**, **subtract**, **find the difference**, **how many more**, **how many less**, **decrease**.

You can use the columnar method to subtract. For example:

H	T	O
8	4	7
− 5	4	3
3	0	4

H	T	O
⁶7̷	¹¹2̷	15
− 2	9	6
4	2	9

Task 1   Use the columnar method to complete these subtractions.

a 836 take away 30.

b Find the difference between 15 and 927.

Task 2

Use the columnar method to complete these subtractions.

a 43 minus 16.

b What is 47 less than 92?

c Subtract 38 from 70.

d Take 53 from 384.

Task 3

Subtract these numbers using the columnar method.

a
```
  738
– 453
```

b
```
  624
–  54
```

c
```
  901
– 690
```

d
```
  834
– 795
```

Exploring Further ...

Three young kangaroos have their jumps measured as shown. Use the columnar method to answer the questions.

1	2	3
203 cm	176 cm	251 cm

a How much further does kangaroo 1 jump than kangaroo 2?

b What is the difference in length between kangaroo 3's jump and kangaroo 1's jump?

Now jump to pages 112–113 to record what you have learned in your Explorer's Logbook.

Multiples

Multiples of a number are the answers in the times table of that number. For example:

2, 4, 6, 8, 10, 12, 14, 16, 18, 20 (and so on) are multiples of 2.

5, 10, 15, 20 (and so on) are multiples of 5.

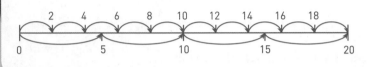

FACT FILE

Animal: Tadpole (baby frog)
Habitat: Just below the surface of shallow water such as lakes, ponds and streams across much of the world
Lifespan: Usually 6 to 9 weeks but for some species the tadpole can take up to 3 years to grow into a frog
Diet: Underwater plants and algae; eats small insects once it is older

WILD FACT

TADPOLES breathe through **GILLS** in a similar way to fish. As they grow, **LUNGS** replace the gills.

| Task 1 | Track down the missing multiples. |

a	18	20			26	28		
b	18			27	30		36	
c		20		28	32		40	
d	15	20				40	45	

Task 2 — Underline the numbers that are:

a multiples of 10: 20 45 54 60 30 100

b multiples of 8: 24 48 80 74 54 96

c multiples of both 4 and 8: 20 8 28 48 32 54

d multiples of both 2 and 3: 9 12 15 20 27 30

e multiples of both 5 and 10: 25 50 60 15 10 45

f multiples of both 50 and 100: 50 150 100 250 200 600

Task 3 — Work out the mystery number in each of these.

a My number is a multiple of 5 and 2.

It lies between 25 and 35. _____

b My number is a multiple of 8. It is a two-digit number.

The two digits add up to make 9. _____

WILD FACT

FROGSPAWN is a mass of **THOUSANDS** of eggs. Each one contains a tiny **TADPOLE** waiting to hatch.

Exploring Further ...

Which frog does each tadpole become?

Tadpole 1 moves left to right along multiples of 8.

Tadpole 2 moves left to right along multiples of 5.

Tadpole 3 moves left to right along numbers that are multiples of both 2 and 3.

1	55	14	15	104	27	18	35	A
2	32	95	36	40	30	85	42	B
3	12	24	88	6	56	16	64	C

Now swim to pages 112–113 to record what you have learned in your Explorer's Logbook.

Multiplication

Multiplication is the repeated addition of a number. It is represented by the sign ×.

6 × 3 can be worked out as 6 sets of 3 (3 + 3 + 3 + 3 + 3 + 3) or 3 sets of 6 (6 + 6 + 6).

If you know the multiplication fact 6 × 3 = 18 or 3 × 6 = 18, it makes life a lot easier – so learn your tables!

Do you know the other words for multiply?

> times, sets of, lots of, product

You should also know written methods of multiplication so that you can deal with bigger numbers. For example, to work out 67 × 3:

The grid method:

	7 ×	60 ×
3	21	180

21 + 180 = 201

So 67 × 3 = 201

The columnar method:

$$\begin{array}{ccc} & T & O \\ & 6 & 7 \\ \times & & 3 \\ \hline 2 & 0 & 1 \\ \hline & 2 & \end{array}$$

FACT FILE

Animal: Hoglet (baby hedgehog)
Habitat: Woodlands, fields, parks and gardens in parts of Europe, Asia and Africa
Weight: 8 to 25 g at birth
Lifespan: Up to 6 years
Diet: Mother's milk for first 4 to 6 weeks, then insects and slugs

Task 1   Answer these to test how well you know your multiplication facts.

a   **i** $3 \times 2 =$ ☐   **ii** $3 \times 5 =$ ☐   **iii** $4 \times 3 =$ ☐   **iv** $6 \times 3 =$ ☐

b   **i** $9 \times 2 =$ ☐   **ii** $5 \times 4 =$ ☐   **iii** $2 \times 8 =$ ☐   **iv** $11 \times 2 =$ ☐

c   **i** $7 \times 4 =$ ☐   **ii** $8 \times 5 =$ ☐   **iii** $7 \times 8 =$ ☐   **iv** $8 \times 3 =$ ☐

Task 2   Complete these multiplications using the grid method.

a 84×8

	$4 \times$	$80 \times$
8		

Answer: _____

b 75×2

	$5 \times$	$70 \times$
2		

Answer: _____

Task 3   Complete these multiplications using the columnar method.

a   89
   ×   5
   _____

b   37
   ×   8
   _____

c   46
   ×   4
   _____

d   94
   ×   3
   _____

Task 4   These questions involve multiplying a multiple of ten.

a $60 \times 8 =$ _____   **b** $80 \times 4 =$ _____   **c** $70 \times 5 =$ _____   **d** $50 \times 4 =$ _____

Exploring Further ...

Answer these by writing down a multiplication sentence for each.

a   A baby hedgehog is 7 cm long. When fully grown it will be four times this length. What length will it grow to?

_____

b   I sketch a hedgehog and make it five times smaller than its real size. If my drawing is 6 cm, what is the size of the real hedgehog?

_____

c   Paul has four anoraks and five scarves for countryside walks. He likes to wear a different combination each time he goes out. How many different outfits can he wear?

_____

Now roll to pages 112–113 to record what you have learned in your Explorer's Logbook.

Division

FACT FILE

Animal: Duckling
Habitat: Ponds, streams and lakes across many parts of the world
Weight: Up to 50 g at birth
Lifespan: 5 to 10 years in the wild
Diet: Insects, worms and aquatic plants

There are two questions you can ask yourself when **dividing**.

Look at the sum 6 ÷ 2.

You can ask: 'What is 6 shared between 2?'

$6 ÷ 2 = 3$

Or you can ask: 'How many sets of 2 in 6?'

$6 ÷ 2 = 3$

Whichever question you ask, the answer will be the same.

For bigger numbers, you will need to know a written method for division, such as:

$$75 ÷ 5 \qquad 5\overline{)7\,^2 5}\;\;{}^{1\;5}$$

WILD FACT

DUCKLINGS do not have **WATERPROOF DOWN,** unlike the adults.

Task 1 — Answer these to test how well you know your division facts.

a **i** 60 ÷ 5 = ☐ **ii** 48 ÷ 8 = ☐ **iii** 20 ÷ 2 = ☐ **iv** 27 ÷ 3 = ☐

b **i** 24 : 4 = ☐ **ii** 24 : 3 = ☐ **iii** 24 : 8 = ☐ **iv** 24 ÷ 2 = ☐

c **i** 35 ÷ 5 = ☐ **ii** 32 ÷ 4 = ☐ **iii** 56 ÷ 8 = ☐ **iv** 40 ÷ 5 = ☐

d **i** 72 ÷ 8 = ☐ **ii** 18 ÷ 3 = ☐ **iii** 16 ÷ 4 = ☐ **iv** 14 ÷ 2 = ☐

Task 2

These questions involve dividing a multiple of 10.

a 80 ÷ 4 = _____   **b** 90 ÷ 3 = _____   **c** 240 ÷ 8 = _____   **d** 300 ÷ 5 = _____

e 400 ÷ 4 = _____   **f** 600 ÷ 3 = _____   **g** 100 ÷ 5 = _____   **h** 350 ÷ 2 = _____

Task 3

Use a written method to solve these divisions.

a 68 ÷ 2

b 93 ÷ 3

c 84 ÷ 2

d 60 ÷ 3

e 92 ÷ 4

f 104 ÷ 8

WILD FACT

It takes about 2 months for **DUCKLINGS** to grow the **FEATHERS** needed for **FLYING.**

Exploring Further ...

Saima, Jack, Millie and Lee went for a picnic. They took 16 sandwiches, 8 apples, 32 grapes, 2 packets of crisps and 4 biscuits. They shared the food equally amongst the four of them. How many of each item did each child receive?

Sandwiches _____   Apples _____   Grapes _____

Packet of crisps _____   Biscuits _____

Now paddle to pages 112–113 to record what you have learned in your Explorer's Logbook.

Money

You need to be able to add and subtract amounts of money.

You should know that there are 100 pence in one pound: 100p = £1. So, for example:

168p = £1 and 68 pence or £1.68
205p = £2 and 5 pence or £2.05

Are you able to work out change?

For example:

You buy a drink that costs 75p using a £1 coin.

You will get 100p – 75p = 25p change.

Task 1

Total each amount of money shown on the fish.

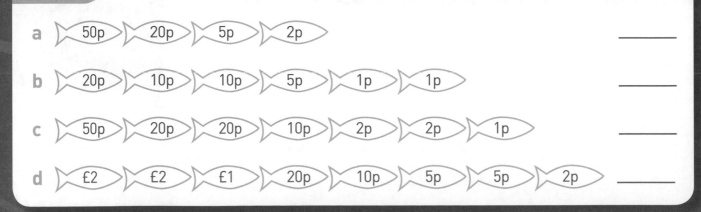

a 50p 20p 5p 2p _____

b 20p 10p 10p 5p 1p 1p _____

c 50p 20p 20p 10p 2p 2p 1p _____

d £2 £2 £1 20p 10p 5p 5p 2p _____

A group of friends go to the souvenir shop after visiting a sealife centre.

Calculate how much each child spends and how much change they each receive.

62p   79p   35p   18p   27p   95p

a Sally buys a pencil and two postcards. She pays with £1.

Spent: _____ Change: _____

b George buys a pencil, a rubber and a postcard. He pays with £1.

Spent: _____ Change: _____

c Alice buys a notebook, a pencil and a keyring. She pays with £2.

Spent: _____ Change: _____

d Saima buys a shark toy, a keyring and a pencil. She pays with £2.

Spent: _____ Change: _____

e Lee buys two shark toys, a pencil and a rubber. He pays with £5.

Spent: _____ Change: _____

WILD FACT

LEMON SHARKS can have up to **18 PUPS.**

Exploring Further ...

Scott, Ismail, Beth and Daisy are going on a fishing trip.

Scott has £6, Ismail has £5.50, Beth has £4 and Daisy has £4.20 to spend.

Before they set off, they each buy a snack to take with them. Scott spends £3, Ismail spends £1 and 10p, Beth spends £1 and Daisy spends 70p.

The fishing trip costs £3.

a Calculate how much each child had left after paying for their snacks.

_____

_____

b Who spent all their money after paying for the fishing?

_____

Now hunt down pages 112–113 to record what you have learned in your Explorer's Logbook.

Straight lines

Straight lines are all around us – on our roads, on our houses, in our books. Straight lines help you to describe shapes and they determine the size of angles.

You must be able to recognise when a line is horizontal ___, or vertical |, or diagonal ╱

When two lines meet at a right angle, they are perpendicular: ∟ or ╋

Parallel lines never meet. Like railway lines, they are the same distance apart right along their length: ═

FACT FILE

Animal: Giraffe calf
Habitat: African savannahs
Weight: Average newborn weighs 50 kg
Lifespan: Up to 25 years
Diet: Mother's milk for up to 17 months but can start eating leaves from 4 months old

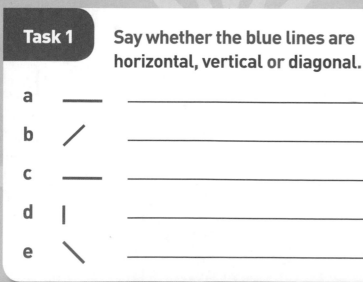

Task 1   **Say whether the blue lines are horizontal, vertical or diagonal.**

a   ___   _____

b   ╱   _____

c   ___   _____

d | _____

e   ╲   _____

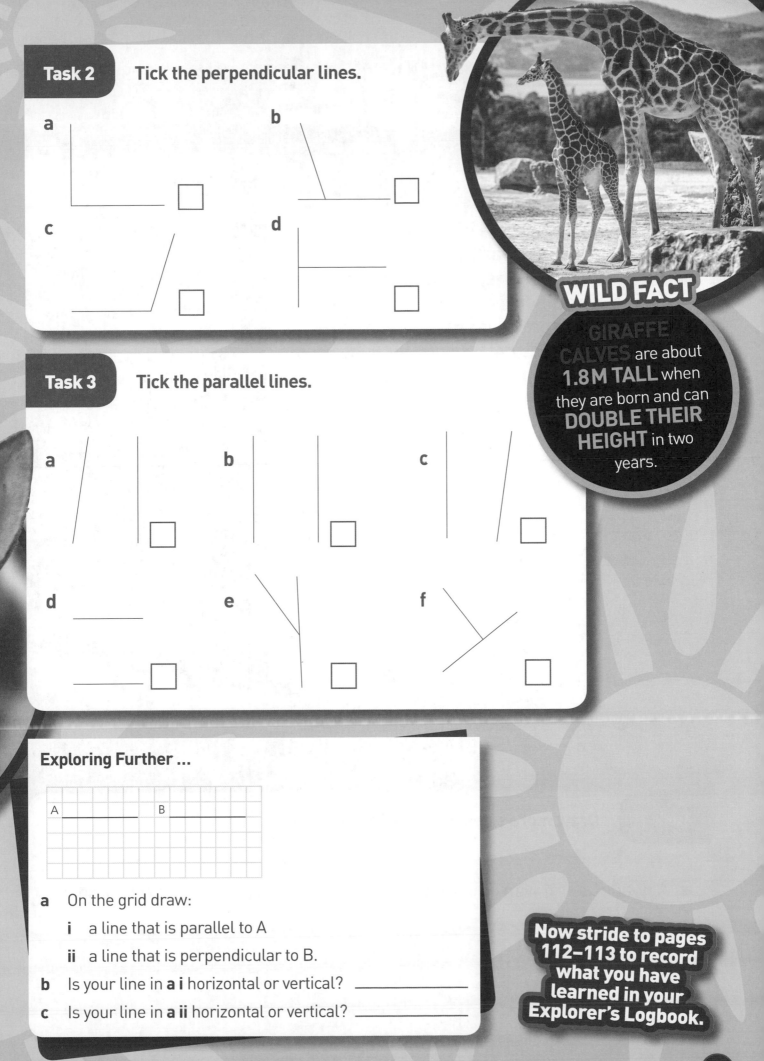

Task 2

Tick the perpendicular lines.

a

b

c

d

Task 3

Tick the parallel lines.

a

b

c

d

e

f

WILD FACT

GIRAFFE CALVES are about **1.8 M TALL** when they are born and can **DOUBLE THEIR HEIGHT** in two years.

Exploring Further ...

A			B						

a   On the grid draw:

   i   a line that is parallel to A

   ii   a line that is perpendicular to B.

b   Is your line in **a i** horizontal or vertical? _____

c   Is your line in **a ii** horizontal or vertical? _____

Now stride to pages 112–113 to record what you have learned in your Explorer's Logbook.

2D shapes

A **2D shape** is a flat shape drawn on a piece of paper. 2D shapes such as triangles, quadrilaterals, pentagons and hexagons are made up of straight sides with angles between them. Sometimes the sides and angles are equal and sometimes they are not. A circle does not have any straight sides.

Check which shapes you can name and see whether you can describe them properly. The first thing to check is how many sides a shape has.

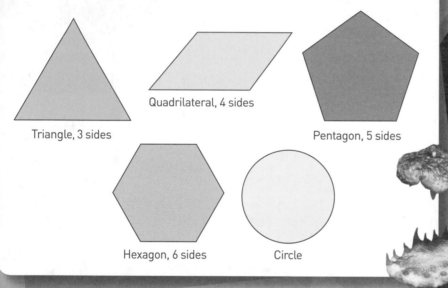

Triangle, 3 sides

Quadrilateral, 4 sides

Pentagon, 5 sides

Hexagon, 6 sides

Circle

Task 1   **Draw more sides to complete these shapes.**

a A quadrilateral with equal sides

b A triangle with one right angle

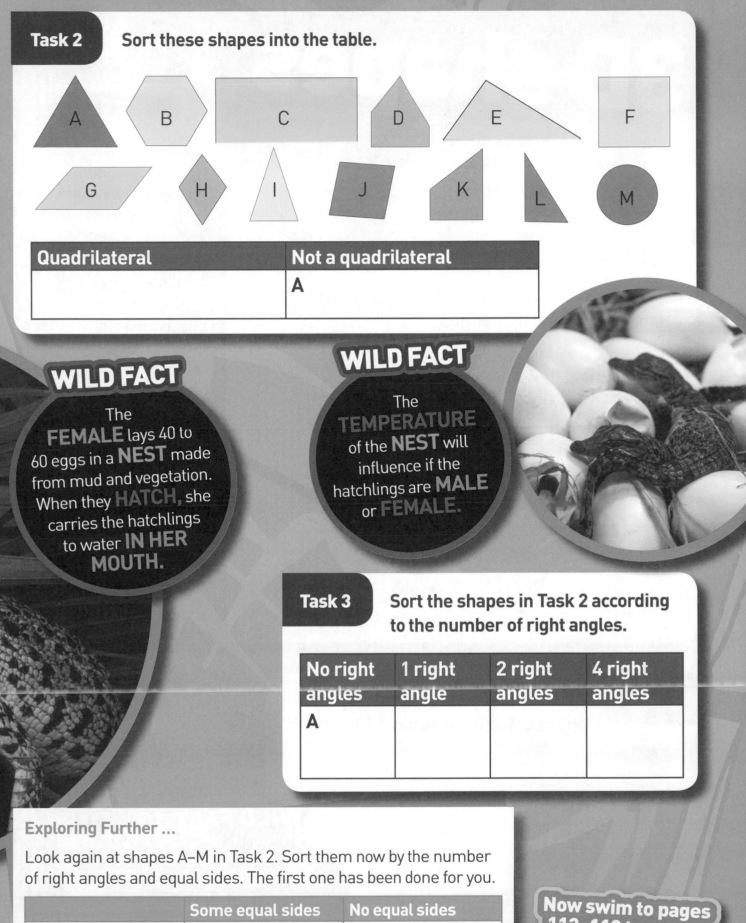

Task 2

Sort these shapes into the table.

Quadrilateral	Not a quadrilateral
	A

WILD FACT

The **FEMALE** lays 40 to 60 eggs in a **NEST** made from mud and vegetation. When they **HATCH**, she carries the hatchlings to water **IN HER MOUTH.**

WILD FACT

The **TEMPERATURE** of the **NEST** will influence if the hatchlings are **MALE** or **FEMALE.**

Task 3

Sort the shapes in Task 2 according to the number of right angles.

No right angles	1 right angle	2 right angles	4 right angles
A			

Exploring Further ...

Look again at shapes A–M in Task 2. Sort them now by the number of right angles and equal sides. The first one has been done for you.

	Some equal sides	No equal sides
One or more right angles		
No right angles	A	

Now swim to pages 112–113 to record what you have learned in your Explorer's Logbook.

3D shapes

A **3D shape** has a length, a width and a height.

3D shapes can be described by how many **surfaces (faces)** they have. Most 3D shapes have **corners (vertices)** and **edges**.

You should be able to name and describe the following shapes:

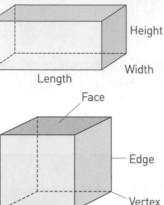

Height
Length
Width
Face
Edge
Vertex

Cube

Cuboid

Sphere

Cylinder

Cone

Square-based pyramid

Triangular prism

Task 1

Here are some pictures of everyday objects. Match the picture to the shape.

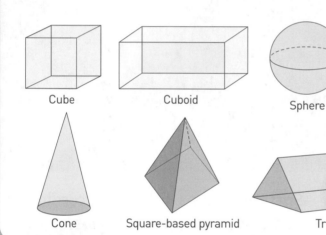

cuboid

cylinder

cone

sphere

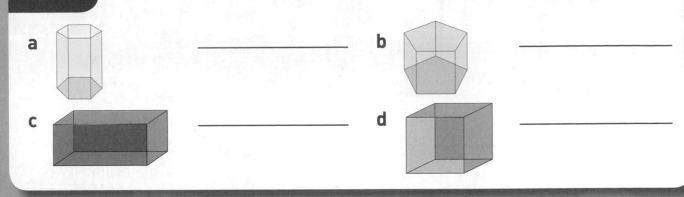

Task 2 What are the names of the shapes on the ends of these prisms?

a _____

b _____

c _____

d _____

Task 3 Complete the table below.

Shape	Faces	Edges	Vertices
Square-based pyramid			
Cylinder			
Pentagonal prism			
Hexagonal prism			

WILD FACT

YOUNG **ORANGUTANS** often stay close to their **MOTHER** for as long as 10 years while they **LEARN** how to **SURVIVE** in the forest.

Exploring Further ...

Here is a model made of a cuboid and a triangular prism.

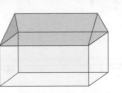

How many faces, edges and vertices does it have?

a faces _____ b edges _____ c vertices _____

Now swing to pages 112–113 to record what you have learned in your Explorer's Logbook.

Number systems

To understand our number system fully, remember that each column is ten times bigger or smaller than the column next to it.

Th	H	T	O
			1
		1	0
	1	0	0
1	0	0	0

A 1 in the tens column is ten times bigger than a 1 in the ones column. It is ten times smaller than a 1 in the hundreds column, and it is 100 times smaller than a 1 in the thousands column.

The Roman number system was more complicated. These were the symbols for one, ten and a hundred:

I = 1 one, X = 1 ten, C = 1 hundred

Here are some more of their numbers. Can you see the patterns?

I = 1	*II = 2*	*III = 3*	*IV = 4*	*V = 5*
VI = 6	*VII = 7*	*VIII = 8*	*IX = 9*	*X = 10*
XI = 11	*XX = 20*	*L = 50*	*C = 100*	

Task 1   Make each of these numbers 10 times greater.

a	T O	b	H T O	c	Th H T O	d	Th H T O	e	Th H T O
	5		9 2		6 8 1		4 0 5		7 9 0
	___		___		___		___		___

Make each of these numbers 10 times smaller.

f	T O	g	H T O	h	Th H T O	i	Th H T O	j	Th H T O
	6 0		2 6 0		5 4 8 0		3 0 1 0		9 5 0 0
	___		___		___		___		___

Task 2 Make each of these numbers 100 times greater.

a 4 _____ b 69 _____ c 29 _____ d 36 _____

Make each of these numbers 100 times smaller.

e 4000 _____ f 3500 _____ g 7100 _____ h 2400 _____

Task 3 What numbers are represented here?

a XV _____

b XXIV _____

c LXI _____

d XC _____

Write these numbers in Roman numerals.

e 16 _____

f 35 _____

g 52 _____

h 26 _____

Exploring Further ...

Which snail did each number on the left go through to become the number on the right?

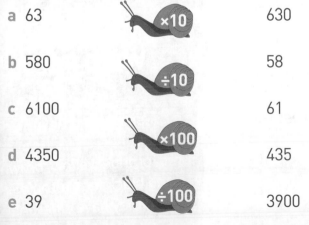

a 63 ×10 630

b 580 ÷10 58

c 6100 ×100 61

d 4350 435

e 39 ÷100 3900

Now creep to pages 114–115 to record what you have learned in your Explorer's Logbook.

Rounding and negative numbers

The **rounding** rules:

- Find the digit to be rounded.
- If rounding to the nearest ten, the digit to be rounded is in the tens column.
- If rounding to the nearest hundred, the digit to be rounded is in the hundreds column, and so on.
- Look at the digit immediately to the right of the digit to be rounded:
  - If it is 0, 1, 2, 3 or 4, the digit to be rounded stays the same.
  - If it is 5, 6, 7, 8 or 9, the digit to be rounded increases by 1.
- So 248 rounded to the nearest hundred is 200 and 248 rounded to the nearest ten is 250.

Negative numbers have a value of less than 0. This number line shows positive and negative numbers:

```
-10   -8   -6   -4   -2   0   2   4   6   8   10
```

| Task 1 | **Round these numbers to the nearest ten.** |

a 23 _____   **b** 78 _____   **c** 35 _____

d 712 _____   **e** 257 _____   **f** 495 _____

Now fly to pages 114–115 to record what you have learned in your Explorer's Logbook.

Task 2

Round these numbers to the nearest hundred.

a 529 _____
b 761 _____
c 350 _____
d 2831 _____
e 7469 _____
f 8963 _____

WILD FACT

The hardened, spotted **WING CASES** that you can see on a **LADYBIRD** protect its **FLYING WINGS** underneath.

Task 3

Round these numbers to the nearest thousand.

a 4449 _____
b 3601 _____
c 7501 _____

Task 4

Complete the following sequences.

a   −4   −3   −2   ____   ____   ____   2   ____

b   ____   ____   ____   −2   0   2   ____   ____

c   −12   −8   ____   ____   4   8   ____   ____

d   ____   ____   ____   −1   4   9   ____   ____

e   −8   ____   ____   1   4   7   ____   ____

Exploring Further ...

Round the numbers on the ladybirds.

	Round to the nearest 10	Round to the nearest 100	Round to the nearest 1000
3117			
5351			
2459			
4965			
4293			
3969			

Factors and multiples

Multiples of a number are found by multiplying that number by another number. For example, the first five multiples of 12 are 12, 24, 36, 48, 60 because:

$12 \times 1 = \mathbf{12}$

$12 \times 2 = \mathbf{24}$

$12 \times 3 = \mathbf{36}$

$12 \times 4 = \mathbf{48}$

$12 \times 5 = \mathbf{60}$

Factors of a number can divide into that number exactly. Factors of a number can be found in pairs that multiply together to make that number.

For example, the factors of 12 are 1, 2, 3, 4, 6, 12 because:

$\mathbf{1} \times \mathbf{12} = 12$

$\mathbf{2} \times \mathbf{6} = 12$

$\mathbf{3} \times \mathbf{4} = 12$

FACT FILE

Animal:	Earthworm
Habitat:	Worldwide under or on the surface of moist soil
Size:	Around 12 cm long
Lifespan:	Certain species can live up to 8 years
Diet:	Decaying roots, leaves and dead animals in the soil

Task 1

These worms are showing numbers that are factors of 30. Draw lines to join one worm to another so that each pair multiplies to get 30.

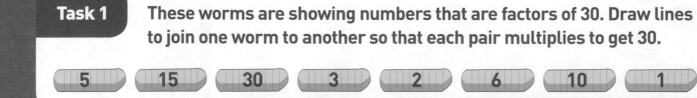

5   15   30   3   2   6   10   1

Task 2 — Track down the missing factors.

a $20 = 4 \times$ _____   b $32 = 8 \times$ _____   c $16 = 2 \times$ _____   d $18 = 6 \times$ _____

Task 3 — Underline the multiples of each emboldened number.

a **6:**	46	36	12	22	18	30
b **7:**	35	42	12	18	28	84
c **9:**	81	56	27	38	72	63
d **25:**	70	50	525	775	485	365

Task 4 — Track down the missing multiples of each emboldened number.

a **1000:**	2000	3000	_____	_____	_____	_____
b **8:**	_____	_____	32	40	_____	_____
c **7:**	_____	21	28	_____	_____	_____
d **9:**	18	_____	36	45	_____	_____

Exploring Further ...

a Write all the factors of each number on the worms' segments:

48

1 | | | | | | | | 48

45

1 | | | | 45

42

1 | | | | | 42

b Which factors do all three worms share? _____

c Which factors are common to 48 and 42? _____

Now wriggle to pages 114–115 to record what you have learned in your Explorer's Logbook.

Fractions

Fractions are a good opportunity to use your knowledge of factors and multiples. You can see from the fractions wall below that $\frac{3}{5}$ is the same as $\frac{6}{10}$.

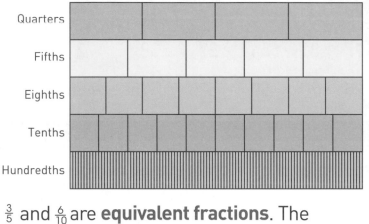

Quarters	
Fifths	
Eighths	
Tenths	
Hundredths	

$\frac{3}{5}$ and $\frac{6}{10}$ are **equivalent fractions**. The top number of a fraction is called the **numerator** and the bottom number of a fraction is called the **denominator**.

Task 1   Use the fractions wall to help you to find equivalent fractions.

a i $\frac{1}{5} = \frac{}{10}$ **ii** $\frac{4}{5} = \frac{}{10}$

   iii Look at each answer. What has the numerator been multiplied by to make the new fraction? _____

b i $\frac{1}{4} = \frac{}{8}$ **ii** $\frac{3}{4} = \frac{}{8}$

   iii Look at each answer. What has the numerator been multiplied by to make the new fraction? _____

c i $\frac{1}{10} = \frac{}{100}$ **ii** $\frac{7}{10} = \frac{}{100}$

   iii Look at each answer. What has the numerator been multiplied by to make the new fraction? _____

Task 2 Use the fractions wall to help you to find equivalent fractions.

a i $\frac{4}{10} = \frac{\;}{5}$ **ii** $\frac{6}{10} = \frac{\;}{5}$

iii Look at each answer. What has the numerator been
divided by to make the new fraction? _____

b i $\frac{4}{8} = \frac{\;}{4}$ **ii** $\frac{6}{8} = \frac{\;}{4}$

iii Look at each answer. What has the numerator been
divided by to make the new fraction? _____

c i $\frac{30}{100} = \frac{\;}{10}$ **ii** $\frac{50}{100} = \frac{\;}{10}$

iii Look at each answer. What has the numerator been
divided by to make the new fraction? _____

WILD FACT

A **HARVESTMAN** looks like a spider but isn't. A spider has two clear body parts, but a **HARVESTMAN** has just **ONE**.

Task 3 Simplify your answers to these fraction sums.

a $\frac{4}{9} + \frac{2}{9} =$ **b** $\frac{7}{8} - \frac{3}{8} =$

c $\frac{5}{12} + \frac{4}{12} =$ **d** $\frac{9}{10} - \frac{3}{10} =$

WILD FACT

The more common name for a **HARVESTMAN** is a 'DADDY LONGLEGS'.

Exploring Further ...

Match a fraction at the end of harvestman A's legs with an equivalent fraction at the end of harvestman B's legs.

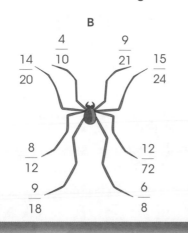

A

$\frac{3}{4}$ $\frac{1}{6}$ $\frac{5}{8}$

$\frac{2}{5}$

$\frac{1}{2}$ $\frac{3}{7}$

$\frac{2}{3}$ $\frac{7}{10}$

B

$\frac{4}{10}$ $\frac{9}{21}$

$\frac{14}{20}$ $\frac{15}{24}$

$\frac{8}{12}$ $\frac{12}{72}$

$\frac{9}{18}$ $\frac{6}{8}$

Now crawl to pages 114–115 to record what you have learned in your Explorer's Logbook.

Decimals

Thousands (Th), hundreds (H), tens (T) and ones (O) all represent whole numbers. In the **decimal system**, a decimal point (.) separates these whole numbers from the fractional part. In the decimal columns, 't' represents tenths and 'h' represents hundredths:

Th H T O . t h

For example:

$0.3 = \frac{3}{10}$ = *three tenths*

$0.03 = \frac{3}{100}$ = *three hundredths*

You must learn these facts:

- ten tenths = 1 whole one
- ten hundredths = 1 tenth
- one hundred hundredths = 1 whole one
- $0.5 = \frac{5}{10} = \frac{1}{2}$
- $0.25 = \frac{25}{100} = \frac{1}{4}$
- $0.75 = \frac{75}{100} = \frac{3}{4}$

Task 1 Write these fractions as decimals.

a $\frac{3}{10}$ _____   b $\frac{7}{10}$ _____   c $\frac{45}{100}$ _____   d $\frac{36}{100}$ _____ e $\frac{1}{2}$ _____

Write these decimals as fractions.

f 0.9   g 0.1   h 0.6   i 0.87   j 0.25

_____   _____   _____   _____   _____

Task 2

Make these numbers 10 times greater. Remember each digit moves one place to the left.

a 3.4 _____ b 5.9 _____ c 7.31 _____ d 4.02 _____

Make these numbers 10 times smaller. Each digit moves one place to the right.

e 61 _____ f 82 _____ g 25.7 _____ h 1.3 _____

Make these numbers 100 times greater.

i 2.64 _____ j 4.92 _____ k 8.3 _____ l 0.2 _____

Make these numbers 100 times smaller.

m 349 _____ n 681 _____ o 56 _____ p 43 _____

Task 3

What is the value of the underlined digit?

a 5.6<u>9</u> _____ b 8.<u>4</u> _____

c 6.0<u>1</u> _____ d 45.1<u>3</u> _____

Task 4

Round these numbers to the nearest whole number.

a 4.2 _____ b 5.9 _____ c 1.5 _____ d 46.3 _____

WILD FACT

The **POND SKATER'S MOUTH** is like a **DAGGER.** It pierces its prey and sucks out the **BODY FLUIDS,** leaving the skin behind.

Exploring Further ...

Which pond skater gets the furthest? Fill the gaps in the table with as many equivalent fractions and decimals as you can from the pond. An example has been done for you.

		0.8	$\frac{8}{10}$	$\frac{80}{100}$	$\frac{4}{5}$	0.80
	a	0.5				
	b	0.1				
	c	0.25				
	d	0.75				
	e	0.7				

$\frac{1}{2}$ $\frac{3}{4}$ $\frac{10}{100}$

$\frac{1}{4}$ $\frac{7}{10}$ 0.70 $\frac{75}{100}$

0.50 $\frac{1}{10}$ $\frac{5}{10}$ $\frac{70}{100}$

$\frac{50}{100}$ 0.10 $\frac{25}{100}$

Now skate to pages 114–115 to record what you have learned in your Explorer's Logbook.

Length

FACT FILE

Animal: Grasshopper
Habitat: Dry, open and grassy places such as meadows and fields
Size: 1 to 7 cm long
Lifespan: 3 to 12 months
Diet: Leaves, flowers, stems and seeds

You need to know how to convert one unit of **length** into another. For example:

10 mm = 1 cm   100 cm = 1 m

Changing from a bigger unit (like a metre) into a smaller one (like centimetres) requires multiplication because there will be more of the smaller units. For example:

$4.34\,m = 4\frac{34}{100}\,m = 4\,m + 34\,cm = 434\,cm$
$4.34\,m = 4.34 \times 100 = 434\,cm$

Converting from a smaller unit to a bigger one requires division. For example:

$86\,mm = 8\,cm + 6\,mm = 8\frac{6}{10}\,cm = 8.6\,cm$
$86\,mm = 86 \div 10 = 8.6\,cm$

WILD FACT

GRASSHOPPERS first lived on EARTH MILLIONS OF YEARS AGO.

Task 1 Write these measures as a fraction of a centimetre and as a decimal fraction of a centimetre, e.g. 3 mm = $\frac{3}{10}$ cm = 0.3 cm

a 1 mm _____

b 7 mm _____

c 9 mm _____

d 21 mm _____

Task 2 Write these measures as a fraction of a metre and as a decimal fraction of a metre, e.g. 17 cm = $\frac{17}{100}$ m = 0.17 m

a 43 cm _____   **b** 57 cm _____

c 21 cm _____   **d** 189 cm _____

Task 3

Perimeter is the distance all the way around the outside.

7 cm

3 cm

The perimeter of this rectangle is
7 cm + 3 cm + 7 cm + 3 cm = 20 cm
OR 2 × (7 cm + 3 cm) = 2 × 10 = 20 cm
The perimeter of a rectangle is often written as
2(length + width).

Find the perimeter of these shapes.

5 cm

4 cm

a

_____

6 cm

2 cm

b

_____

3 m

3 m

c

_____

Task 4

Area is how much space is within a 2D shape. Count the squares to find the area of each shape.

a

_____

b

_____

Exploring Further ...

The average length of creatures in two different habitats was compared. In the first habitat, the lengths were measured in millimetres (mm) and in the second habitat the lengths were measured in centimetres (cm). Help out by finding the difference in average length of each creature in mm and cm.

	First habitat	Second habitat	Difference in mm	Difference in cm
Centipede	15 mm	2 cm		
Woodlouse	25 mm	2.7 cm		
Earthworm	85 mm	7 cm		
Millipede	19 mm	2.5 cm		
Grasshopper	57 mm	4.3 cm		

Now hop to pages 114–115 to record what you have learned in your Explorer's Logbook.

FACT FILE

Animal:	Aphid
Habitat:	On plants in gardens and fields worldwide
Size:	1.5 to 3.5 mm long
Lifespan:	7 to 40 days
Diet:	Plant juices

Can you remember key facts about **mass**?

1000 mg = 1 gram, 1000 g = 1kg, 1000 kg = 1 t

When converting between different measures of mass, you only need to think about sets of a thousand. For example:

5912 g = 5 kg + 912 g = 5 kg 912 g

6 t 12 kg = 6000 kg + 12 kg = 6012 kg

Take care with your place value in these conversions.

Task 1   Match each animal to the most appropriate measure of mass.

elephant   dog   aphid

0.2 milligrams   13 kilograms   3 tonnes

Task 2   Change these measures into kilograms and grams, e.g. 3910 g = 3 kg 910 g.

a 2731 g _____   b 5802 g _____

c 6091 g _____   d 4400 g _____

Change these measures into tonnes and kilograms, e.g. 2841 kg = 2 t 841 kg.

e 9263 kg _____   f 4905 kg _____

g 8012 kg _____   h 3200 kg _____

Task 3

Change these measures into grams, e.g. 3 kg 40 g = 3040 g.

a 5 kg 500 g _____

b 8 kg 86 g _____

c 4 kg 9 g _____

d 2 kg 349 g _____

WILD FACT

APHIDS pierce plant stems and **SUCK** the **SAP.** This can weaken the plant.

Task 4

Change these measures into milligrams, e.g. 9 g 9 mg = 9009 mg.

a 8 g 274 mg _____

b 3 g 700 mg _____

c 5 g 24 mg _____

d 7 g 2 mg _____

Task 5

Put these masses in order, starting with the heaviest.

a 721 g   721 kg   7210 g   7 kg 2 g   7201 kg   7 t 70 kg

_____

b 4035 mg   4 g   4003 g   4 g 5 mg   3 kg 54 g   3045 g

_____

Exploring Further ...

a A biologist has calculated that 175 000 aphids would weigh just 35 grams. Show this mass on the scale below.

0 g ————————————— 50 g ————————————— 100 g

b The biologist also studied some aphids found in a fossil. She marked the mass of the fossil on the scale below. Round the mass to the nearest kilogram.

0 kg —— 1 kg —— 2 kg —— 3 kg —— 4 kg —— 5 kg

_____

WILD FACT

When **APHIDS POO,** they leave a **STICKY SUBSTANCE** on the plant.

Now turn to pages 114–115 to record what you have learned in your Explorer's Logbook.

Capacity

FACT FILE

Animal: Stick insect
Habitat: Worldwide in forests and grasslands
Size: Up to 33 cm long
Lifespan: Up to 3 years in the wild
Diet: Leaves, plants and berries

The standard unit of **capacity** is the **litre**. There are 1000 ml in one litre. There is also a measure of capacity called the **centilitre**. You will not come across it very often but you need to know that:

- *100 centilitres = 1 litre*
- *10 ml = 1 centilitre.*

WILD FACT

STICK INSECTS have excellent CAMOUFLAGE, meaning that they blend into the twigs and leaves of their surroundings.

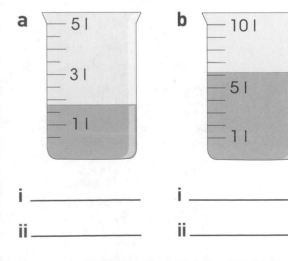

Task 1

Look at these containers. What is:
i   the exact reading?
ii the reading to the nearest litre?

a
— 5 l
— 3 l
— 1 l

i _____

ii _____

b
— 10 l
— 5 l
— 1 l

i _____

ii _____

Task 2

Look at these containers. How many centilitres need to be added to make 1 litre?

a
— 1 l
— 50 cl
— 10 cl

_____

b
— 1 l
— 50 cl
— 10 cl

_____

Task 3

How much needs to be taken out of each container to make 500 ml?

a

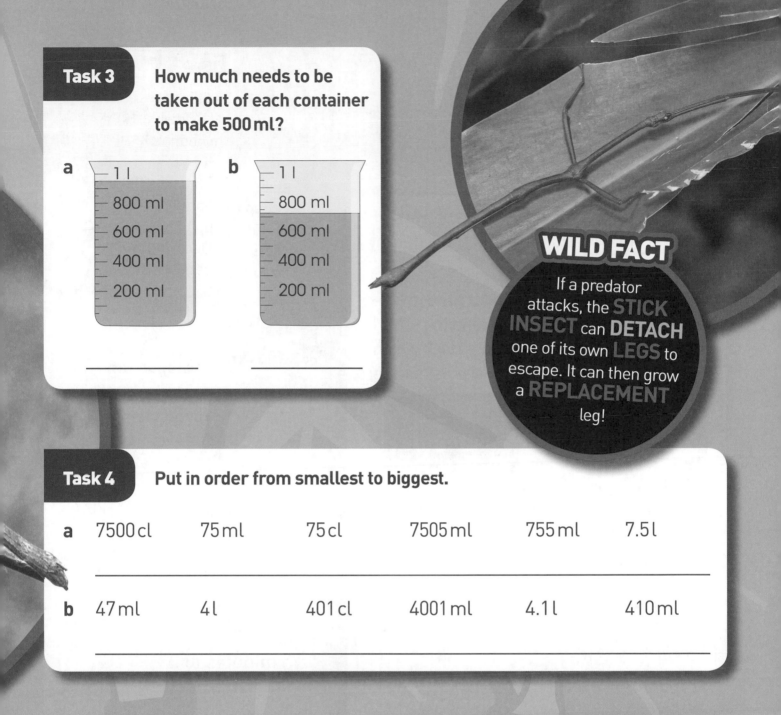

- 1 l
- 800 ml
- 600 ml
- 400 ml
- 200 ml

b

- 1 l
- 800 ml
- 600 ml
- 400 ml
- 200 ml

WILD FACT

If a predator attacks, the STICK INSECT can DETACH one of its own LEGS to escape. It can then grow a REPLACEMENT leg!

Task 4

Put in order from smallest to biggest.

| **a** | 7500 cl | 75 ml | 75 cl | 7505 ml | 755 ml | 7.5 l |

| **b** | 47 ml | 4 l | 401 cl | 4001 ml | 4.1 l | 410 ml |

Exploring Further ...

Match the pairs which make 2 litres together.

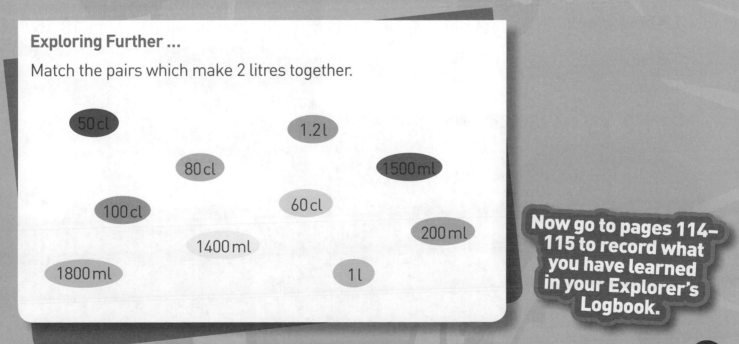

50 cl

1.2 l

80 cl

1500 ml

100 cl

60 cl

200 ml

1400 ml

1800 ml

1 l

Now go to pages 114–115 to record what you have learned in your Explorer's Logbook.

Time

FACT FILE

Animal:	Millipede
Habitat:	Worldwide beneath wood, rocks, leaves or in soil
Size:	0.5 to 35 cm long
Lifespan:	Some species can live up to 10 years
Diet:	Decaying wood and vegetation

Make sure you know the different ways of reading and writing **time** and the different units used.

Analogue time is when you read the time from a clock with moving hands.

Digital time is when you read the time from a clock which only shows numbers.

Check your facts:

60 seconds = 1 minute

60 minutes = 1 hour

24 hours = 1 day

7 days = 1 week

12 months = 1 year

12-hour clock	**24-hour clock**
6.30 am	*06:30*
10.15 pm	*22:15*

Task 1 — Match the analogue time on the left with the correct digital time on the right.

5 past 6 in the morning	20:45
quarter to 9 in the evening	06:05
quarter past 3 in the afternoon	07:54
25 minutes to 2 in the afternoon	15:15
6 minutes to 8 in the morning	13:35

WILD FACT

The name **MILLIPEDE** means **'A THOUSAND FEET'**, but no millipede has that many feet. They have **TWO PAIRS OF LEGS** on each **SEGMENT** of their body.

| Task 2 | Write these 12-hour clock times as 24-hour clock times. |

a 11.43 pm _____   **b** 11.21 am _____   **c** 8.13 am _____

d 6.57 pm _____   **e** 1.25 pm _____

| Task 3 | Mrs Higham says, 'Our train arrives at 19:35.' Which children are correct? |

Peter says, 'That's 25 to 7 in the evening.'

Paula says, 'No, that's 7.35 in the evening.'

Philip says, 'No, it's 25 to 8 in the evening.'

Patricia says, 'No, it's 35 minutes past seven in the evening.'

_____

WILD FACT

When in danger, **MILLIPEDES** curl up and some give off a **SMELLY LIQUID** from **GLANDS** on their **SIDES**.

| Task 4 | Solve these calculations. |

a How many minutes are there in 7 hours?   _____

b How many seconds are there in 30 minutes?   _____

c How many months are there in 9 years?   _____

d How many days are there in 8 weeks?   _____

Exploring Further ...

Write the numbers in these sentences in a more useful way.

a The millipede's eggs hatched 84 days after being laid.

The millipede's eggs hatched _____ weeks after being laid.

b A millipede can live for 96 months.

A millipede can live for _____ years.

c It took me 240 seconds to find some millipedes in my garden.

It took me _____ minutes to find some millipedes in my garden.

Now crawl to pages 114–115 to record what you have learned in your Explorer's Logbook.

Angles

An angle is a measure of turn. Angles are created when two straight lines meet or cross and they are measured in degrees (°).

- A **right angle** (a quarter turn) measures 90°.

- A **straight line** (a half turn) is equal to two right angles or 180°.

- An angle which is smaller than a right angle (less than 90°) is called **acute**.

- An angle which is bigger than a right angle but less than two right angles (more than 90° but less than 180°) is called **obtuse**.

acute

obtuse

right angle

straight line

Task 1

State whether each marked angle is acute, obtuse or a right angle.

a

b

c

d

_____   _____   _____   _____

Task 2

State whether each of these angles is acute, obtuse or a right angle.

a 36° _____   b 91° _____

c 175° _____   d 90° _____

e 12° _____   f 87° _____

Task 3

Put these angles in order of size, starting with the smallest.

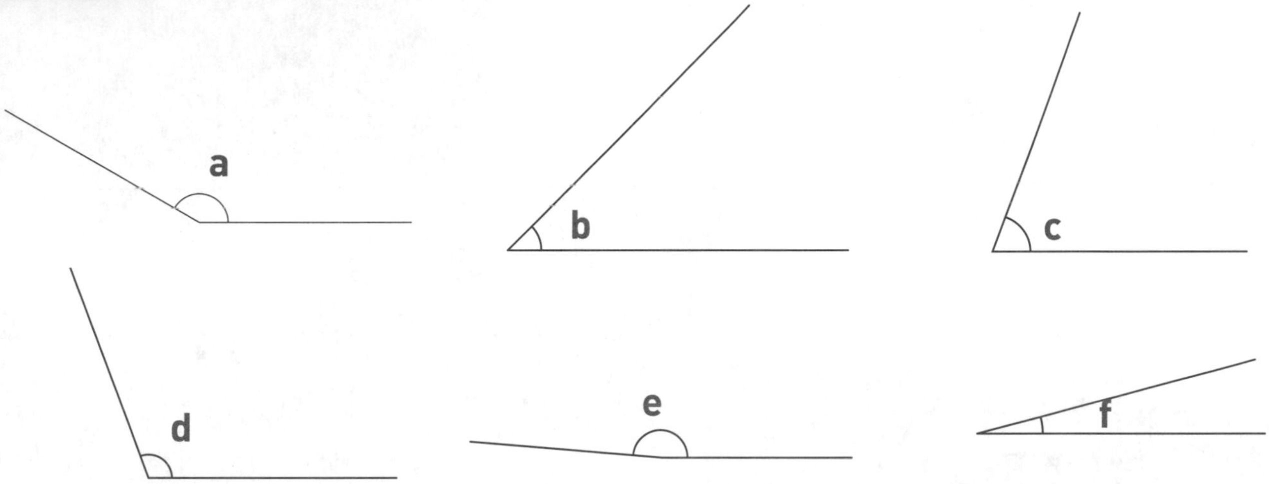

_____

Exploring Further ...

State whether the angles in each of the following shapes are equal or unequal.

a

_____

b

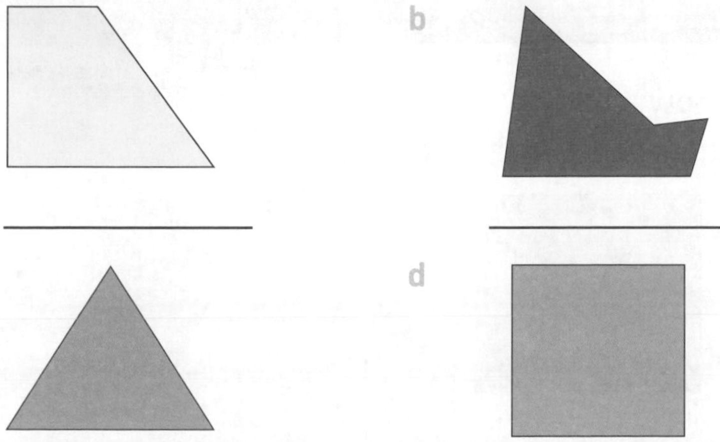

_____

c

_____

d

_____

Now turn to pages 114–115 to record what you have learned in your Explorer's Logbook.

Symmetry

Shapes are **symmetrical** when you can fold them in half and both halves match exactly.

The line of the fold is called the line of symmetry and is often shown as a dotted line.

Did you know?

The wings of a butterfly are symmetrical!

 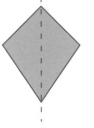

FACT FILE

Animal: European peacock butterfly
Habitat: Around flowers in gardens, parks and meadows in Europe and parts of Asia
Size: Average wingspan of 6 to 6.5 cm
Lifespan: About 11 months
Diet: Flower nectar, rotten fruit and tree sap

Task 1 Does each dotted line show a line of symmetry on these shapes? Answer yes or no.

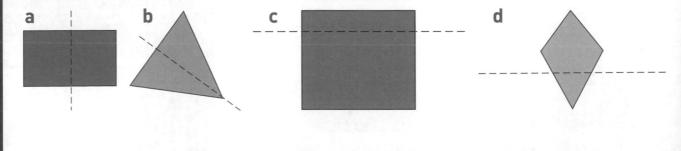

a   b   c   d

_____   _____   _____

Task 2

Which of these shapes are symmetrical? Put a tick in the box.

a

b

c

d

☐ ☐ ☐ ☐

Task 3

Colour more blocks to make symmetrical patterns.

WILD FACT

CATERPILLARS hatch from butterfly eggs and they spin a **SILKY TENT** around themselves. This acts as **PROTECTION** while each caterpillar develops into a pupa and later emerges as a butterfly.

Exploring Further ...

Complete the shapes in all four parts of the grid by reflecting them each way in the lines of symmetry.

Now flutter to pages 114–115 to record what you have learned in your Explorer's Logbook.

Coordinates & translations

Shapes can be moved by sliding them up or down and right or left. When a shape is moved in this way without turning or changing it, it is called a **translation**.

Coordinates describe a shape's position. The cross on this grid is at the coordinate (5, 4). The first number describes how far along and the second number describes how far up or down.

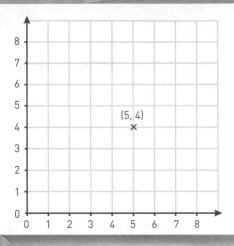

(5, 4)

Task 1

Give the coordinates of each scorpion fly.

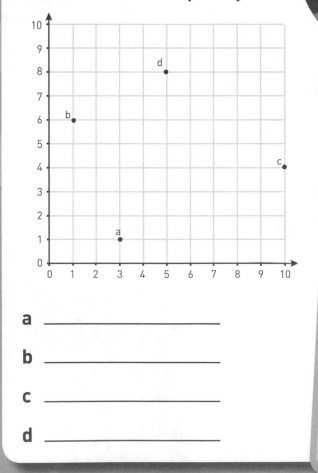

a _____

b _____

c _____

d _____

FACT FILE

Animal: Scorpion fly
Habitat: Hedgerows, nettles and woods worldwide
Size: Up to 30 mm in length; wingspan of 35 mm
Lifespan: Up to 1 year
Diet: Dead insects, nectar, pollen and fruit

Task 2

Describe the movement of the scorpion fly (S). State how many squares left or right it needs to move and then how many squares up or down it needs to move to reach its food (F).

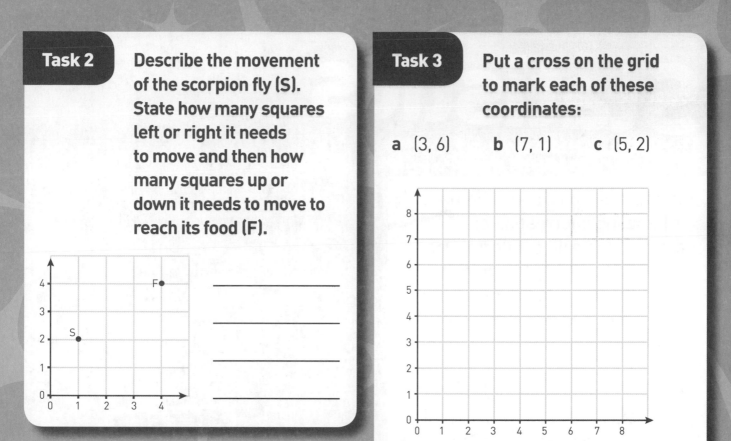

_____

_____

_____

_____

Task 3

Put a cross on the grid to mark each of these coordinates:

a (3, 6) **b** (7, 1) **c** (5, 2)

WILD FACT

A male **SCORPION FLY** may give a **DEAD INSECT** to a female in order to attract her attention.

WILD FACT

Unlike a real scorpion, the **SCORPION FLY** does not use its tail to sting. In fact it does **NOT KILL ANYTHING**, preferring to eat **DEAD INSECTS**.

Exploring Further ...

Plot the following points:
A (2, 5), B (8, 5), C (2, 2).
With a ruler, join A to B and A to C. Point D will complete a rectangle. Give the coordinates of point D and complete the rectangle.

Point D is _____

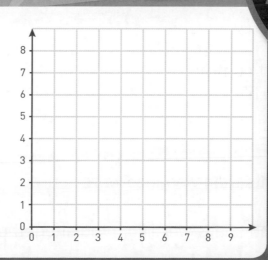

Now fly to pages 114–115 to record what you have learned in your Explorer's Logbook.

Statistics

Statistics is a part of mathematics for handling information or **data**. You can collect information on almost anything – how many children in your class like certain TV programmes, how fast your friends can run 100m, the numbers of birds visiting a garden, and so on. The information collected can be presented in various ways to make it easier to understand and to make conclusions about it.

FACT FILE

Animal: Horsefly
Habitat: Worldwide in fields and hedgerows near water
Size: 8 to 23mm
Lifespan: A few days as an adult fly
Diet: Females: mammals' blood; males: nectar

Task 1

Year 3 counted how many different kinds of creatures they could find in the school garden in 15 minutes. They presented their results in this bar chart:

a Which was the most common type of creature seen?

_____

b Which was the least common type of creature seen?

_____

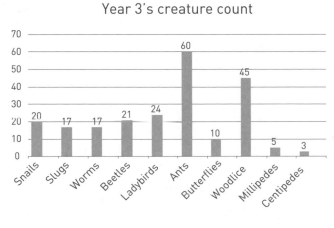

Year 3's creature count

c How many more ants than woodlice were counted? _____

d How many slugs and snails were counted altogether? _____

Task 2

Year 4 conducted a survey of aphids on the class geranium plant. Every Monday they counted how many aphids they could see and then made monthly totals.

They made this line graph of their results:

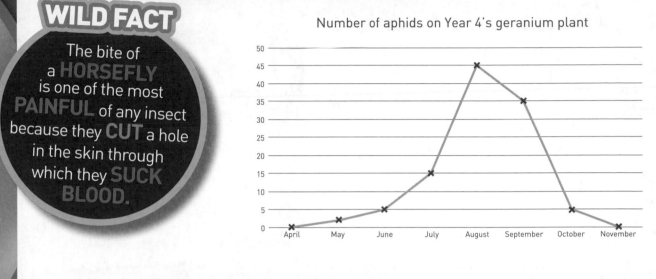

Number of aphids on Year 4's geranium plant

a In which month were most aphids seen? _____

b How many more aphids were counted in August than in September? _____

c In which month was the number of aphids the same as in June? _____

d In which month was the number of aphids 20 more than in July? _____

Exploring Further ...

Rhianna and George went pond dipping. They decided to make a bar chart from their findings. Rhianna has entered her results.

Draw the bars for George's results (below) on the same chart, below each of Rhianna's bars.

Caddis fly larva: 2
Pond skater: 7
Water boatman: 11
Diving beetle: 3

Which creature did they count most of altogether?

Pond dipping survey

_____

Now go to pages 114–115 to record what you have learned in your Explorer's Logbook.

Homophones

Words that **sound the same** but have **different meanings and spellings** are called **homophones**. They can be easy to mix up so you have to be careful to use the correct word.

Look at these examples:

whale   *wail*

WILD FACT

BLUE WHALES are believed to be the **LARGEST ANIMAL EVER TO HAVE LIVED.**

Task 1 **Circle the correct word to complete each sentence.**

a Whales spend most of <u>there/their/they're</u> lives swimming alone.

b I hoped to see a whale but I could not find <u>won/one</u>.

c Whales can <u>here/hear</u> each other up to 1600 km away.

d The whale was <u>two/too/to</u> far away for me to see clearly.

e Whales do have <u>hare/hair</u> but only a very small amount.

f Whales use their <u>tails/tales</u> to slap the water.

Task 2   Write a homophone for each of these words.

a due _____

b groan _____

c son _____

d great _____

e pair _____

f bear _____

WILD FACT

The **TONGUE** of a **BLUE WHALE** can weigh as much as an **ELEPHANT** and its **HEART** as much as a **CAR!**

Task 3   Write a sentence using each of these words.

a sea _____

b see _____

c for _____

d four _____

e where _____

f wear _____

Exploring Further ...

Unscramble these pairs of homophones.

a lera _____   eler _____

b frloo _____   lwaf _____

c igrht _____   ewitr _____

d lueb _____   lwbe _____

e neba _____   ebne _____

Now jump to pages 116–117 to record what you have learned in your Explorer's Logbook.

Word families

Being able to spot words that belong in the same **family** can help you to work out **what they mean** and **how they are spelt**.

Words in the same family often share similar **letter patterns**.

Look at these examples:

real   really   realistic   reality

FACT FILE

Animal: African bush elephant
Habitat: The savannah, deserts and rainforests of Africa
Weight: Up to 10000 kg
Lifespan: Up to 70 years
Diet: Roots, grasses, fruit and bark

WILD FACT

AFRICAN BUSH ELEPHANTS are the largest LAND-DWELLING MAMMALS and the second tallest after the giraffe.

Task 1   Sort these words into families. Write each family in a leaf.

unsafe   reapply   familiarity   safety   apply   application

unfamiliar   safest   familiarise

Task 2 Add two words that would belong to the same family as each of the words shown.

a contain _____ _____

b regret _____ _____

c allow _____ _____

d follow _____ _____

Task 3 Work out these words. They are all from the same family. Some letters have been given to help you.

a football p l __ __ __ r

b school p __ __ y __ __ __ __ __ __ d

c __ l __ y f __ __ __ puppy

d __ __ a __ i __ g tennis

Exploring Further ...

Find these related words in the wordsearch grid.

V	A	L	A	V	U	E	D	L
D	L	L	E	A	L	N	E	D
B	E	V	A	L	U	A	T	E
S	U	A	S	U	V	A	E	U
V	A	L	U	A	B	L	E	L
T	T	U	W	T	B	I	D	A
L	U	E	E	I	C	L	M	V
O	E	R	T	O	T	I	E	L
Y	D	L	M	N	L	L	V	E

value

valuable

valuation

evaluate

valued

WILD FACT

AFRICAN BUSH ELEPHANTS live in **GROUPS** guided by the **OLDEST FEMALE**, called the **MATRIARCH.** She decides when the group rests, bathes and drinks.

Now charge to pages 116–117 to record what you have learned in your Explorer's Logbook.

ch words

The letters **ch** can make **different sounds**, even in easier words. Try reading these words out loud:

school   chihuahua   chef

Getting to know words like this will make them easier to read and spell.

Task 1   Find and copy two words from the box in which the **ch** sound matches each given word.

mechanic	chill	chandelier
brochure	echo	charm

a chair

_____   _____

b monarch

_____   _____

c chalet

_____   _____

Task 2   Colour the correctly spelt word in each pair of bones.

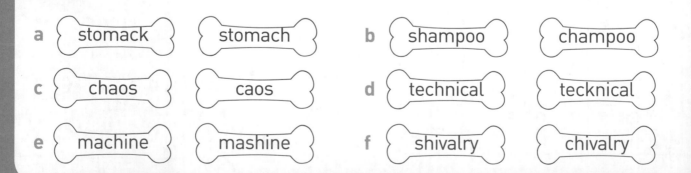

a stomack / stomach   **b** shampoo / champoo

c chaos / caos   **d** technical / tecknical

e machine / mashine   **f** shivalry / chivalry

a choir_____

_____

b chauffeur_____

_____

c which_____

_____

d scheme_____

_____

e chip_____

_____

f charge_____

_____

WILD FACT

The **CHIHUAHUA** is the **SMALLEST** breed of dog. They are named after the **MEXICAN STATE** in which the breed first appeared.

WILD FACT

CHIHUAHUAS tend to tremble when they are excited, worried or cold. **SHORT-HAIRED** types may need a jumper or boots to stay **WARM.**

Exploring Further ...

Add the missing letters to complete these **ch** words. Use the picture clues to help you.

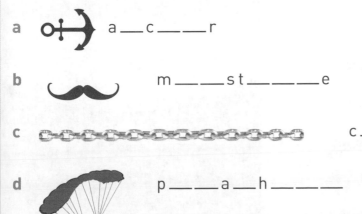

a a __ c __ __ __ r

b m __ __ s t __ __ __ __ e

c c __ __ __ __ __

d p __ __ __ a __ h __ __ __

Now run to pages 116–117 to record what you have learned in your Explorer's Logbook.

65

y or i?

Animal:	Western pygmy blue butterfly
Habitat:	Scrubby grassland and desert in North and Central America
Weight:	Almost nothing!
Lifespan:	Adult butterflies live for around a week
Diet:	Nectar

Some words which sound like they are spelt with an **i** actually contain a **y**, like this creature's name:

western <u>pygmy</u> blue butterfly

You need to learn these words and remember how to spell them.

Task 1 Add y or i to complete these words.

a   m __ stery

b   h __ story

c   rh __ thm

d   r __ ddle

e   hab __ t

f   prett __ ly

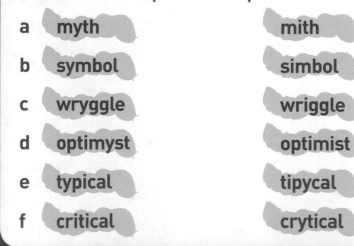

Task 2 Circle the correctly spelt word in each pair of caterpillars.

a   myth   mith

b   symbol   simbol

c   wryggle   wriggle

d   optimyst   optimist

e   typical   tipycal

f   critical   crytical

Task 3 — Draw a line from each word to its meaning.

a cymbals   beats in a word

b anonymous   round metal musical instrument

c syrup   of unknown name

d syllable   Australian animal

e platypus   thick, sticky sugary liquid

WILD FACT

The **WESTERN PYGMY BLUE BUTTERFLY** is one of the world's **SMALLEST** butterflies, with a **WINGSPAN** of just **20 MM.**

WILD FACT

The **WESTERN PYGMY BUTTERFLY** sucks up flower **NECTAR** through a mouthpart that looks like a tiny **STRAW.**

Exploring Further ...

Find these words in the wordsearch grid.

E	D	N	O	E	L	E	A
D	K	L	O	G	A	M	P
S	O	N	E	I	P	C	H
S	Y	M	P	H	O	N	Y
X	L	S	K	O	A	L	S
O	N	Y	T	X	D	J	I
W	O	P	S	E	N	O	C
A	L	Y	D	I	M	Y	A
A	M	L	E	A	Y	A	L

symphony

physical

system

onyx

lynx

Now flutter to pages 116–117 to record what you have learned in your Explorer's Logbook.

67

ou words

The letters **ou** can make the same sound as **u** in some words.

For example, read this word out loud:

enough

Task 1 Add u or ou to complete each word.

a disc__rage

b n__rish

c b__rrow

d b__nting

e t__gh

f wr__ng

g h__ng

h sp__rt

Task 2 Underline a spelling mistake in each sentence. Write the correct word on the line.

a Explorers show currage in exploring new places. _____

b I saw a cupple of goliath frogs hopping along. _____

c African goliath frog tadpoles flurrish in fast streams. _____

d The explorer went to a lot of trubble to find the frog. _____

e She travelled over rugh territory searching for it. _____

Task 3 Add the missing letters to complete a word that rhymes with each of these.

a much   t _ _ _ _

b rubble   d _ _ _ _ _ _

c tongue   y _ _ _ _

d cuff   r _ _ _ _

Task 4 These words have the letters **ou** missing from them. Write the words again, with **ou** in the right place.

a jeals _____

b fams _____

c hazards _____

d fabuls _____

e nervs _____

f varis _____

g obvis _____

h curis _____

Exploring Further ...

Write one sentence using all three of these words.

country   encourage   youngest

_____

_____

_____

Now hop to pages 116–117 to record what you have learned in your Explorer's Logbook.

Apostrophes

Animal:	Falabella miniature horse
Habitat:	Originally bred on the plains of Argentina
Weight:	18 to 45 kg
Lifespan:	Up to 45 years
Diet:	Grass and hay

Apostrophes do an important job. They can be used to show that something belongs to someone or something.

If you are writing about **one person or thing**, the apostrophe goes before the **s**, like this:

A horse's hooves

If you are writing about more than one person or thing, the apostrophe usually goes after the **s**, like this:

Two horses' hooves

Some plurals do not end in **s**. With these words, the apostrophe goes before the **s** like this:

The men's saddles

Task 1   Add an apostrophe to each phrase.

a an explorers notebook

b the suns warmth

c two scientists discoveries

d three horses tails

e all of the ladies hats

f a mares food

g a grey ponys mane

h two childrens hats

WILD FACT

The **FALABELLA** is one of the **SMALLEST BREEDS** of horse in the world.

Task 2 Turn the singular nouns into their plurals. One is done as an example.

Singular	Plural
horse's ear	*horses' ears*
man's hat	
child's toy	
baby's rattle	
woman's book	
person's vote	
animal's foot	

WILD FACT

FALABELLAS can be used to help people in the same way as a **GUIDE DOG** because they are so small and can be **TRAINED** easily.

Task 3 Is the apostrophe in the correct place in these sentences? Tick **yes** or **no** for each one.

a Peoples' love of Falabellas means they are famous across the world.   **yes** ☐   **no** ☐

b A Falabellas' tiny hoof prints could be seen at the edge of the forest.   **yes** ☐   **no** ☐

c This books' photographs show Falabellas of different colours.   **yes** ☐   **no** ☐

d The horses' coat has a beautiful pattern.   **yes** ☐   **no** ☐

e The trainer's goal was to teach her Falabella to pull the cart.   **yes** ☐   **no** ☐

Exploring Further ...

Write TRUE or FALSE next to each statement.

a With a singular noun, the apostrophe always goes before the **s**. _____

b With plural nouns, the apostrophe always goes after the **s**. _____

c With words like *people* and *children*, the apostrophe goes before the **s**. _____

Now trot to pages 116–117 to record what you have learned in your Explorer's Logbook.

More apostrophes

Apostrophes can also be used when letters are taken out to join two words together in a contracted form, like this:

was not   *wasn't*

The apostrophe replaces the letter or letters that have been removed.

| **Task 1** | Draw lines to match up the pairs of words with the correct contracted form. |

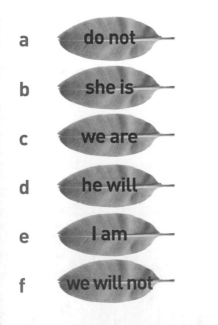

a   do not   I'm

b   she is   we're

c   we are   we won't

d   he will   don't

e   I am   she's

f   we will not   he'll

FACT FILE

Animal:	Speckled padloper tortoise
Habitat:	Rocky areas in South Africa
Weight:	95 to 165g
Lifespan:	Unknown
Diet:	A variety of plants, especially wild flowers

Task 2

Write down the contracted form for each of these phrases.

a should not _____

b they are _____

c will not _____

d are not _____

e we would _____

f you are _____

Task 3

Write down the letter or letters that each apostrophe has replaced.

a she'll _____

b they'd _____

c can't _____

d it's _____

e they're _____

f it'll _____

WILD FACT

The **SPECKLED PADLOPER TORTOISE** is the world's **SMALLEST TORTOISE.** It is less than **11CM** long.

Exploring Further ...

Insert the full form of these contracted words in the crossword grid.

Across

2. it'd

3. couldn't

4. I've

5. we've

Down

1. should've

Now crawl to pages 116–117 to record what you have learned in your Explorer's Logbook.

Word endings

The word endings **sion**, **ssion**, **cian** and **tion** all sound very similar. For example, try reading these words out loud:

expansion   profession   mathematician   rejection

You need to learn which ending to use. You will discover that **tion** is the most common ending.

Task 1

Add the correct ending to each word. Use the clues to help you.

a man _____ (a big house)

b pa _____ (strong feelings)

c opti _____ (fits spectacles)

d electri _____ (fixes wiring)

e pen _____ (income in old age)

f permi _____ (allowing something)

Task 2 Colour the correctly spelt word in each pair of shells.

a mician | **mission**

b confecian | **confession**

c **tension** | tencian

d **musician** | musision

e politission | **politician**

f **extension** | extencian

WILD FACT

Lots of other creatures, like **CRABS, SHRIMP AND FISH,** live in and around **GIANT BARREL SPONGES.**

Task 3 Write a sentence using these words.

a action _____

_____

b discussion _____

_____

c comprehension _____

_____

d magician _____

_____

Exploring Further ...

Unscramble these words. Some letters have been given to help you.

a VEINTOINN   I _ _ _ _ _ T _ _ _ _

b SISODAMIN   _ D M _ _ _ S _ _ _ _

c ATRONI   R A _ I _ _

Now take in pages 116–117 to record what you have learned in your Explorer's Logbook.

Punctuation

Punctuation marks help readers to understand your writing.

Full stops, question marks and exclamation marks at the end of a sentence help to show what kind of sentence it is.

Commas separate items in a list or show you where to pause when reading.

Inverted commas go before and after direct speech, to show that someone is speaking.

Task 1 Add a full stop, question mark or exclamation mark to these sentences.

a A pygmy marmoset is about 15 cm long

b Have you ever seen a pygmy marmoset

c Those monkeys are totally amazing

d Have you discovered where marmosets live

e A pygmy marmoset is the world's smallest monkey

Task 2   Add the missing commas to these sentences.

a   The pygmy marmoset feasted on sap leaves and berries.

b   The explorer packed water food a map and a compass for the journey.

c   You find out about wildlife from zoos libraries and websites.

d   Pygmy marmosets are found in Brazil Peru Colombia and Ecuador.

e   The pygmy marmoset is prey for cats eagles hawks and snakes.

WILD FACT

The **LOWER TEETH** of **PYGMY MARMOSETS** are adapted to **CARVE HOLES** in **TREE BARK** to get at the sap, gum or resin underneath.

Task 3   Add the missing inverted commas to these sentences.

a   There's a marmoset in that tree! exclaimed the explorer.

b   I managed to take a photograph of it, replied the wildlife photographer.

c   The explorer commented, That will look great in our logbook.

d   I'll see if I can take another one, added the photographer.

e   I can count nine marmosets in that tree! said Akemi.

Exploring Further ...

Add the missing punctuation to this passage.

The explorers trekked into the forest They saw colourful birds tiny frogs and large snakes

Look up there shouted their guide Can you see the marmosets in the trees

Now leap to pages 116–117 to record what you have learned in your Explorer's Logbook.

Tenses

Tenses tell you whether something is happening **now**, happened in the **past** or will happen in the **future**, like this:

I explore   I explored   I will explore

When you write, make sure that you are using the right tense all the way through.

WILD FACT

The **BARBADOS THREADSNAKE** is thought to be the world's **SMALLEST** snake. It is just over **10 CM** long and about as thin as a strand of spaghetti.

Task 1

Complete the table by filling in the past tense verbs. The first one has been done for you.

Present tense	Past tense
walk	*walked*
search	
bring	
wake	
live	
sleep	

WILD FACT

Scientists only learned about **BARBADOS THREADSNAKES** in **2008**, so relatively **LITTLE IS KNOWN** about them.

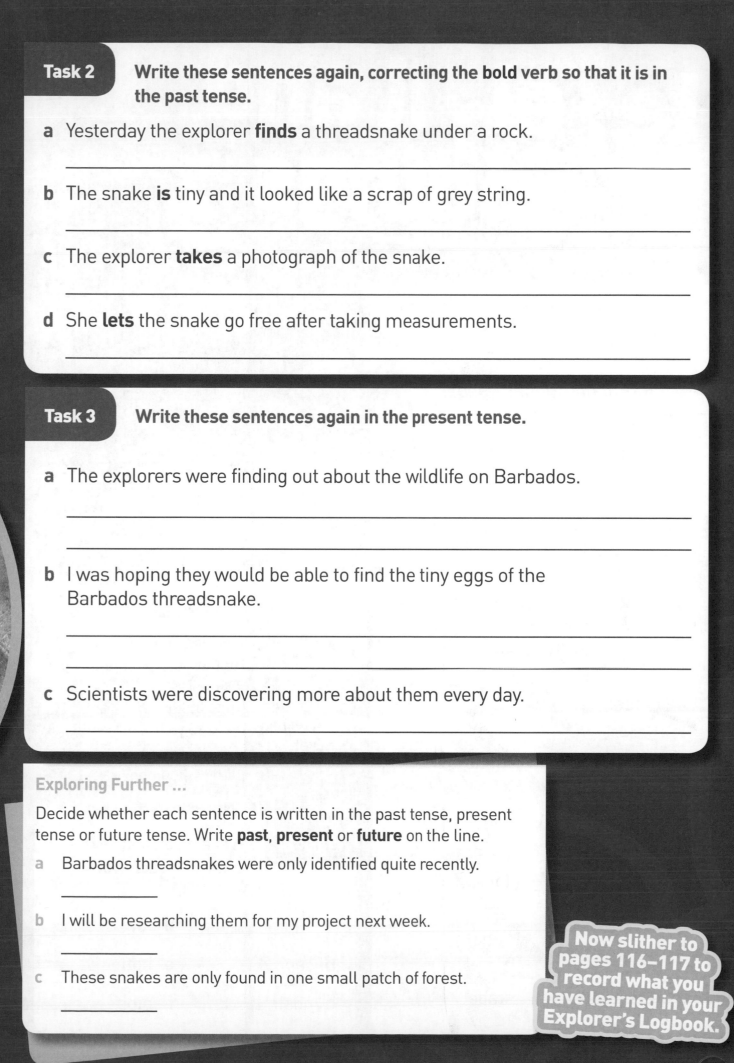

Task 2 Write these sentences again, correcting the **bold verb** so that it is in the past tense.

a Yesterday the explorer **finds** a threadsnake under a rock.

_____

b The snake **is** tiny and it looked like a scrap of grey string.

_____

c The explorer **takes** a photograph of the snake.

_____

d She **lets** the snake go free after taking measurements.

_____

Task 3 Write these sentences again in the present tense.

a The explorers were finding out about the wildlife on Barbados.

_____

_____

b I was hoping they would be able to find the tiny eggs of the Barbados threadsnake.

_____

_____

c Scientists were discovering more about them every day.

_____

Exploring Further …

Decide whether each sentence is written in the past tense, present tense or future tense. Write **past**, **present** or **future** on the line.

a Barbados threadsnakes were only identified quite recently.

_____

b I will be researching them for my project next week.

_____

c These snakes are only found in one small patch of forest.

_____

Now slither to
pages 116–117 to
record what you
have learned in your
Explorer's Logbook.

le, el, il and al endings

The word endings **le**, **el**, **il** and **al** all sound very similar. For example, say these words out loud:

battle   tunnel   lentil   pedal

These similar sounds can make words tricky to spell. You need to learn which words have each ending.

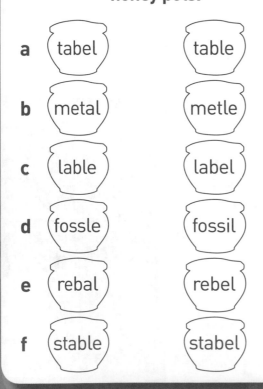

Task 1

Colour the correctly spelt word on each pair of honey pots.

a tabel   table

b metal   metle

c lable   label

d fossle   fossil

e rebal   rebel

f stable   stabel

Task 2

Write el, al, il or le to complete each word.

a squirr _____   d tow _____

b capit _____   e bott _____

c nostr _____   f nibb _____

Task 3 Underline the mistake in each sentence. Write the correct word on the line.

a Explorers traval to faraway places to find out about animals.

_____

b The explorer tracked the animel into the trees.

_____

c In the middel of the forest, the sun bear climbed a tree.

_____

d A littal bear cub was curled up in the branches.

_____

e The wind rocked the branches like a cradel.

_____

WILD FACT

SUN BEARS are the world's SMALLEST bear. Despite their name, they are NOCTURNAL.

WILD FACT

SUN BEARS are also known as HONEY BEARS. They have a really long TONGUE, so they can get honey out of bees' nests.

Exploring Further …

Use the picture clues to help you complete the crossword grid.

Across

1.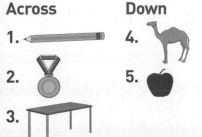

2.

3.

Down

4.

5.

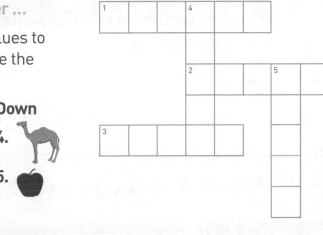

Now roam to pages 116–117 to record what you have learned in your Explorer's Logbook.

More tenses

Tenses are a way to change verbs to help you describe when something is done. If you are writing about something that happened in the past and is finished, you can use the **simple past**. For example:

The salamander stayed at the edge of the river for hours.

If you are writing about something that started in the past but still carries on, you can use the **present perfect tense**. For example:

The salamander has stayed at the edge of the river for hours.

WILD FACT

The world's largest amphibian, the **CHINESE GIANT SALAMANDER** grows up to **1.8 M IN LENGTH.**

FACT FILE

Animal:	Chinese giant salamander
Habitat:	Mountain streams and lakes of China
Weight:	20 to 25 kg
Lifespan:	Unknown in the wild but up to 60 years in captivity
Diet:	Aquatic insects, fish, frogs, crabs and shrimp

Task 1   **Underline the present perfect verb form in these sentences. Look at the example above to help you.**

a Scientists have studied giant salamanders for years.

b The numbers of Chinese giant salamanders in the wild have fallen.

c They have cared for Chinese giant salamanders in zoos.

d An archaeologist has found the fossil of a Chinese giant salamander.

e People have seen these salamanders in underground river systems.

Task 2 **Tick the sentence that includes the present perfect verb tense.**

a The giant salamander hid in the murky water. ☐

b The explorer photographed a Chinese giant salamander. ☐

c Relatives of the salamander have existed on Earth for millions of years. ☐

WILD FACT

CHINESE GIANT SALAMANDERS make a noise which sounds so like a **CRYING CHILD** that they are known as **'INFANT FISH'** in Chinese.

Task 3 **Write these sentences again, replacing the verb in bold with the present perfect tense.**

a A female salamander **laid** 500 eggs in a stream.

_____

b A male salamander **looked** after the eggs.

_____

c Conservation workers **protected** the salamanders' habitat.

_____

Exploring Further ...

Find the simple past forms of these present perfect verbs in the wordsearch grid. The first one has been found for you.

has written

has seen

has known

has run

has left

has woken

W	L	A	E	K	W
A	R	A	N	J	E
S	S	O	A	E	K
L	E	A	T	L	O
R	K	K	N	E	W
U	N	E	C	F	K
N	E	S	W	T	Q

Now crawl to pages 116–117 to record what you have learned in your Explorer's Logbook.

Plurals

Plurals allow you to write about more than one thing but there are spelling rules you need to know.

To turn most nouns into a plural, you just add **s**:

animal ——→ animals

If the noun ends in **s**, **sh**, **x**, **zz**, or **ch**, you add **es**:

bush ——→ bushes

For words ending in a consonant followed by **y**, remove the y and add **ies**:

baby ——→ babies

With words ending in **f**, you usually remove the f and add **ves**:

wolf ——→ wolves

Some words change completely when they are plural:

mouse ——→ mice

Some words do not change at all!

sheep ——→ sheep

Task 1 Write the plural of each of these nouns.

a explorer _____

b fox _____

c wish _____

d pebble _____

e lady _____

f monkey _____

Task 2   Circle the correct plural in each pair.

a **shelf**	shelfs	shelves
b **pony**	ponies	ponys
c **deer**	deers	deer
d **man**	men	mans
e **life**	lifes	lives
f **foot**	feet	foots

WILD FACT

AFRICAN PYGMY MICE are one of the **SMALLEST** types of rodent in the world.

Task 3   Sort these words into the table depending on how you turn them into plurals.

poppy   witch   loaf   leaf   party   forest

discovery   half   glass   creature   key   bus

Add *s*	Add *es*	Remove the *y* and add *ies*	Remove the *f* and add *ves*

Exploring Further ...

Unscramble these plural nouns, then draw lines to match them with the correct singular noun.

a	NHRLICDE	_____	goose
b	TTEHE	_____	louse
c	LEOPPE	_____	tooth
d	EEGES	_____	child
e	ELCI	_____	person

Now scurry to pages 116–117 to record what you have learned in your Explorer's Logbook.

Syllables

A **syllable** is the single unit of sound used to make up a word or part of a word. A word with one syllable is called **monosyllabic**, such as:

sea, crab

A word with two syllables is called **disyllabic**, such as:

limpet (lim-pet), rockpool (rock-pool)

A word with three or more syllables is called **polysyllabic**, such as:

jellyfish (jell-y-fish), submarine (sub-ma-rine)

An easy way to count syllables is to clap along with the word as you say it slowly.

Task 1	Count how many syllables are in these words and write the number in the box.

a earth ☐   **b** accident ☐

c circle ☐   **d** special ☐

e anemone ☐   **f** ocean ☐

g strength ☐   **h** peculiar ☐

i pressure ☐   **j** unidentified ☐

Task 2

Add the missing syllables to complete each word.

a _____a_____   Definition: A musical keyboard.

b _____tory   Definition: The study of the past.

c _____en_____   Definition: Look at this to find out the day, month and year.

d Ex_____i_____   Definition: A scientific procedure.

Task 3

Think of a word for each definition.

a Monosyllabic word _____
Definition: Pump in the body that keeps blood circulating.

b Disyllabic word _____
Definition: A way to describe someone or something well-known.

c Disyllabic word _____
Definition: People always 'on the go' and bees are described as this.

d Polysyllabic word _____
Definition: The opposite of forget.

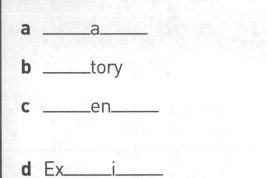

WILD FACT

Some **ANEMONES FIGHT EACH OTHER** by striking out with their **TENTACLES!**

Exploring Further ...

Say what you see in each picture below, and count the syllables. Join each picture to the correct rockpool.

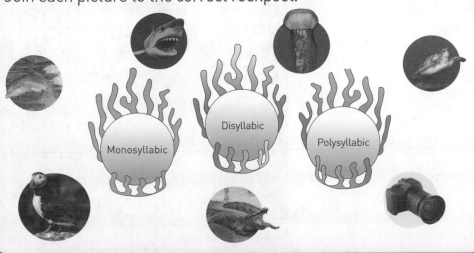

Monosyllabic

Disyllabic

Polysyllabic

Now grab pages 118–119 to record what you have learned in your Explorer's Logbook.

Phonemes

Now we are going to look at some different ways of writing the same **sound**. Sounds in words are called **phonemes**. When you learn to read, you often sound out the phonemes, for example:

f-l-a-g = flag   *l-i-f-t-s = lifts*

Some sounds are represented by more than one letter, for example:

'qu' and 'ir' in 'squirt', or 'ch' and 'air' in 'chair'

A **grapheme** is how the phoneme is written. Some phonemes can be written using different letters:

The phoneme 'ee' can be written 'ee' as in 'tree'; 'ea' as in 'beat'; 'ie' as in 'chief'; or 'ei' as in 'ceiling'.

Task 1

Choose the correct grapheme from the options given in brackets and complete the word.

a   ca _____ (**tch / ch**)

b   cli _____ (**m / mb**)

c   (**kn / nn**) _____ it

d   (**r / wr**) _____ ong

e   (**n / kn / gn**) _____ ear

f   pin _____ (**ch / tch**)

g   (**ch / c / ck**) _____ emist

h   (**f / ph / ff**) _____ one

i   (**n / kn**) _____ owledge

j   le _____ (**j / dge**)

Task 2

The following words have the wrong long vowel grapheme. Write the word with its correct grapheme.

fr**oo**t		w**a**t**e**	
g**i**d**e**		wr**oa**t	
br**y**t		compl**ea**t	
gr**oo**p		br**ie**the	
b**e**d**e**		extr**ea**m	

Task 3

Circle the word whose phoneme is said differently in each set.

a **ch**imp   s**ch**ool   **ch**eat   **ch**ill   su**ch**

b w**eigh**t   h**eigh**t   fr**eigh**t   n**eigh**bour   **eigh**teen

c peng**ui**n   g**ui**de   acq**ui**re   q**ui**et   inq**ui**re

d sw**a**llow   **a**rrive   c**a**lendar   **a**crobat   pl**a**nkton

e br**ea**th   s**ea**   ah**ea**d   d**ea**th   l**ea**ther

WILD FACT

SEA SQUIRTS are FILTER FEEDERS, which means they live off TINY PARTICLES and ORGANISMS they have filtered from the water.

Exploring Further ...

Complete the crossword using the clues. Make sure you choose the correct grapheme!

Across

1. Coral _____

4. Long-tentacled sea creature

5. 12 months

6. Another word for Earth

Down

2. The animal featured on this page

3. Type of feeder a sea squirt is

Now squirt to pages 118–119 to record what you have learned in your Explorer's Logbook.

Prefixes

A **prefix** can be a group of letters or a short word. Adding a prefix to the **start** of a word changes the meaning of the word. Look at these examples:

legal   ⟶   _il_legal

possible   ⟶   _im_possible

regular   ⟶   _ir_regular

expensive   ⟶   _in_expensive

The prefixes **il**, **im**, **ir** and **in** change the meaning of the word to the **negative** or **opposite** meaning. Now work through the tasks and discover the rules!

Task 1   Sort these words by their prefixes into the correct nests.

illogical	irregular	illiterate	indescribable	immature
impersonal	irreplaceable	invalid	improbable	irrational

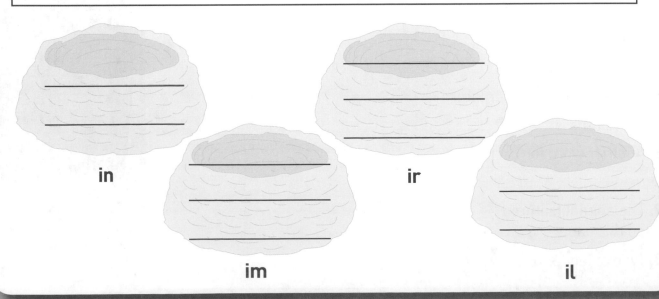

in

im

ir

il

Task 2

Look at the words in Task 1 again. Match a box in the left column with a box in the right column to create a set of rules.

Use **il** for words that	begin with 'l'
Use **ir** for words that	begin with 'm' or 'p'
Use **im** for words that	begin with all other letters
Use **in** for words that	begin with 'r'

Task 3

Now apply your rules to the following words to check they work.

Root word	Add correct prefix
legal	
correct	
responsible	
formal	
expensive	
visible	
possible	

WILD FACT

The **ALBATROSS** is the only bird that can **FLY 16000KM (10000 MILES)** **WITHOUT LANDING.**

WILD FACT

ALBATROSSES have the **LONGEST WINGSPAN** of any bird – up to **3.5M.**

Exploring Further ...

Starting at 'in', colour in a path across the grid by joining a prefix to an appropriate root word in an adjoining box. What is the longest path you can make?

in	active	im	legible	in	correct
il	migrant	possible	ir	polite	il
formal	in	il	legal	im	right
ir	im	expensive	ir	luminate	in
patient	correct	im	regular	il	relevant
responsible	il	in	patient	adequate	im

Now glide to pages 118–119 to record what you have learned in your Explorer's Logbook.

Suffixes

A **suffix** is a group of letters added to the **end** of a word to change its meaning. We will look at the suffix **ous**. This changes a word into an **adjective**, for example:

adventure ⟶ adventur<u>ous</u>

If the word ends in **ge**, keep the **e** and add **ous**, for example:

outrage ⟶ outra<u>geous</u>

If the word ends in **y**, change it to **i** and add **ous**, for example:

fury ⟶ fur<u>ious</u>

Task 1	**Change each word to an adjective by adding ous.**

a victory _____

b nerve _____

c danger _____

d glory _____

e courage _____

f poison _____

Task 2 Change the root word in brackets to an adjective to complete the sentence.

a You should be _____ around sea urchins. (**caution**)

b The spines of the sea urchin may be

_____ . (**venom**)

c Sea urchins are _____ for their coats of sharp spines. (**fame**)

d Sea urchins are not found in

_____ regions. (**mountain**)

e Sea urchins are found in _____ sizes, depending on the water temperature of the ocean they live in. (**vary**)

WILD FACT

Certain species of **SEA URCHIN** have **SPINES** filled with **VENOM!**

Task 3 These two words do not follow the rules given in the introduction. Can you explain the rules for adding the suffix **ous** to these words?

glamour ⟶ glamorous   disaster ⟶ disastrous

_____

_____

Exploring Further ...

Turn the words stuck in the urchins' spikes into adjectives by adding **ous**. Write the new word on the line.

infection

ambition

_____

hazard

mystery

_____   _____

Now tread carefully to pages 118–119 to record what you have learned in your Explorer's Logbook.

Delivering details

FACT FILE

Animal:	Dogfish
Habitat:	The coastlines of the Atlantic Ocean, Pacific Ocean and Indian Ocean
Weight:	3 to 5 kg; the maximum recorded weight was 9.8 kg!
Lifespan:	25 to 80 years
Diet:	Fish, squid and crustaceans

One of the easiest ways to make your writing more interesting to the reader is to add lots more information about the things you are mentioning. 'The dogfish ...' may not sound all that interesting, but 'The venomous, spiny dogfish . . .' may get your attention! Adding **adjectives** in this way creates an **expanded noun phrase**. You can also add detail at the beginning of the sentence by adding a short phrase called a **fronted adverbial**. It is followed by a comma, then the rest of the sentence. For example:

The dogfish swam away + fronted adverbial =

Without warning, the dogfish swam away.

WILD FACT

The **SPINY DOGFISH** is a species of **SHARK**. It is also commonly known as the piked dogfish, the codshark and the thorndog.

Task 1

Put a circle around the nouns. Underline the verbs and cross out the adjectives.

bird   fish   man

deadly   poisonous

smooth   crawl   crab

patterned   sleep

swim   swoop

Task 2

Draw a line to join up the sentence sections that you think should go together.

Gently,   I go swimming.

Once a week,   he leapt forward.

Suddenly,   I love to read.

On holiday,   he lifted up the baby.

Task 3

Below are different sections of sentences. Colour sections in the same colour to make an interesting or funny sentence!

The small, hairy

The talented

The overgrown

The spiny

The strict

teacher

tarantula

garden   performer   dogfish

climbed the tree.

migrated south.

needed tidying up.

sat at the desk.   sang beautifully.

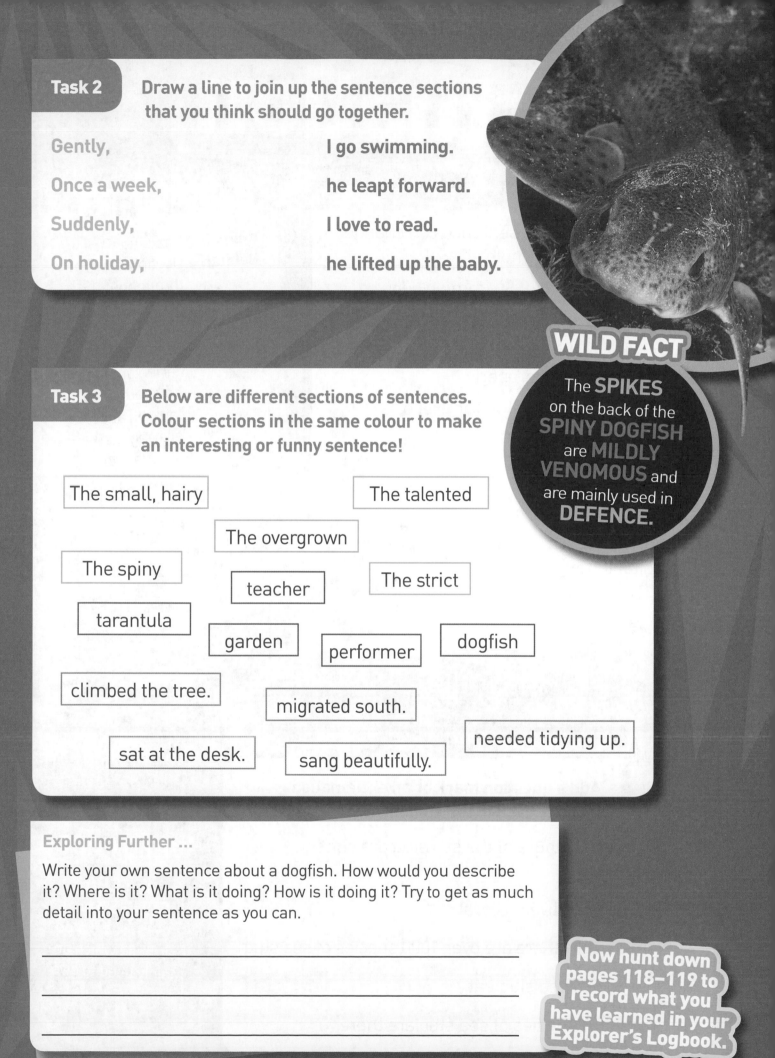

WILD FACT

The **SPIKES** on the back of the **SPINY DOGFISH** are **MILDLY VENOMOUS** and are mainly used in **DEFENCE.**

Exploring Further ...

Write your own sentence about a dogfish. How would you describe it? Where is it? What is it doing? How is it doing it? Try to get as much detail into your sentence as you can.

_____

_____

_____

Now hunt down pages 118–119 to record what you have learned in your Explorer's Logbook.

Punctuation

How you **punctuate** a sentence can change its **meaning**. For example:

Private property? No! Swimming allowed.

Private property. No swimming allowed.

Make sure you know how to use these punctuation marks properly:

- Speech marks: "Hello," or 'Hello,'
- Exclamation mark: **!**
- Question mark: **?**
- Full stop: **.**
- Comma: **,**
- Capital letter: **A**
- Apostrophe: don't

Task 1	Add a question mark or an exclamation mark to each of the sentences.

a The bright colours of the sea slug are simply amazing

b Do sea slugs live on coral

c Remarkably, there are over 1000 species of sea slug

d How does a sea slug eat

e How many species of sea slug are there

Apostrophes can be used to show where a letter is missing. Choose a single word to replace the words in brackets. The first one has been done for you.

(**It is**) _____It's_____ the amazing sea slug! It may look like sea slugs (**do not**) _____ have teeth, but in fact they do – (**they are**) _____ just tiny. Predators (**are not**) _____ always able to spot sea slugs that are camouflaged against the seabed or rocks. Some species (**can not**) _____ be seen because they blend in so well with the surrounding seaweed. (**I have**) _____ never seen a real sea slug – have you?

WILD FACT

SEA SLUGS come in all sorts of wonderful **SHAPES, COLOURS AND SIZES.**

Task 3

Correct these sentences and add punctuation marks.

a more than 500 species of sea slug live on australias great barrier reef

_____

_____

b didnt you know that sea slugs can regenerate parts of their body

_____

_____

c brilliant ive seen a sea slug thought the scuba diver

_____

Exploring Further ...

Punctuation bingo!

With a friend, take turns to read sentences from a book. Cross out the punctuation on your board when you come across it!

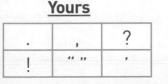

Yours

.	,	?
!	" "	'

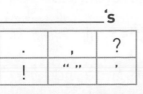

_____'s

.	,	?
!	" "	'

Now squirm to pages 118–119 to record what you have learned in your Explorer's Logbook.

Conjunctions

When writing for an audience, it is important that you include all of the **detail** necessary. You should also use varied vocabulary and smoothly flowing sentences, in a way that keeps the reader **interested**.

One simple way to improve the quality of your writing is to combine two short sentences into one longer, more interesting one. To do this you use **conjunctions**. These are words that join ideas within a sentence, such as:

but, yet, therefore, since, rather, nor

Task 1 Complete the sentences by choosing the most appropriate conjunction from the brittle star's arms. Use each one only once.

a The brittle star has five arms _____ its central body part is roughly pentagonal in shape.

b Its arms are covered in sharp spines, _____ these are very fragile.

c The brittle star can be hard to spot _____ it is well camouflaged.

d It is also known as the 'serpent star' _____ it has snake-like movements.

e Many other animals hunt the brittle star, _____ it spends much of its time hidden.

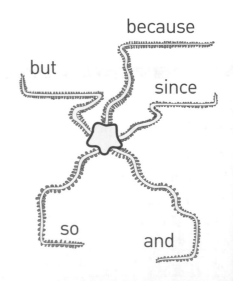

because

but

since

so

and

Task 2 — Use three different colours to add full stops, insert capital letters and to circle any words that are spelt incorrectly.

brittle stars can be found in sees all over the world they have teeny bodies and five long arms with spiky bits on them brittle stars can break off these arms to escape meat-eating animals that hunt them the arms quickly grow back in some species brittle stars can move fast in any direction usin there arms like legs some people call them serpent stars coz they think they move like snakes they are hard to spot as they manely come out at night

Task 3 — Some of the vocabulary in the passage above could be improved. Look at the words below and choose a replacement word from the box.

carnivorous	regenerate	small	predators	nocturnal

a   teeny

b   animals that hunt

c   grow back

d   meat-eating

e   come out at night

Exploring Further ...

Use your best handwriting to rewrite the paragraph from Task 2 on a separate piece of paper, adding punctuation, correcting spelling mistakes and changing some of the words used to improve it. Show your finished writing to someone to read and see how much you can teach them about the brittle star.

Now make your way to pages 118–119 to record what you have learned in your Explorer's Logbook.

How do you know?

On these pages, you are going to improve your ability to **infer** and **deduce** about moods and feelings. In pictures, or with words, characters often reveal how they feel, even if they may not use the actual words to express how they are feeling. For example:

A character might not say, "I am feeling worried," but they may be described as fidgeting, or perhaps hesitating in speech.

So you can deduce a character's feelings by using other clues, including body language, speech and description.

Task 1   Draw lines to match the feeling word with the picture.

happy   surprised

upset   grumpy   worried

WILD FACT

The **JAPANESE SPIDER CRAB** can measure as much as **5.5 M FROM CLAW TO CLAW!**

Task 2

Read these extracts and write two words to describe the character's mood. Underline any words or phrases that help you deduce the feeling.

a "I really wanted to go to the beach today," the boy said with a glum face. "But can we go tomorrow instead?"

How was he feeling? _____ _____

b The children crept towards a rockpool and cautiously looked over the edge. The bottom wasn't visible from the surface.
"Are you sure we need to find it?" asked the girl.

How was she feeling? _____ _____

c The little boy raced across the beach, his bucket swinging wildly. Suddenly, he stopped, and then poked a large pebble with his toe.
"Got one, Dad!" he yelled.

How was the boy feeling? _____ _____

Task 3

Look at the comic strip below and describe how the characters are feeling.

I'm glad that question about spider crabs came up...

I can't believe I forgot to feed the fish!

a _____   b _____

WILD FACT

The **ARMOUR-LIKE** features of the **JAPANESE SPIDER CRAB'S** body help to **PROTECT** it from larger predators such as octopuses.

Exploring Further ...

Draw a character and write a speech bubble for it. Can a friend or parent guess the feeling of your character?

Now pick out pages 118–119 to record what you have learned in your Explorer's Logbook.

What happens next?

A fun thing to do when you are reading a book can be to stop halfway through a sentence and **think**, 'I wonder what will happen next?' Maybe you can **predict** what a character will do or how the story will end.

WILD FACT

PUFFINS are **EXCELLENT FLIERS**. Flapping their wings at up to **400 BEATS PER MINUTE**, they can reach speeds of 88 KM/H (55 MPH).

Task 1	Look at how each of these facts start and draw a line to connect it to the correct ending.

a

The puffin's bright orange bill has led to it being nicknamed...	the 'sea parrot' and 'bottlenose'.
	the 'monkey-sloth' and 'kangaroo-bear'.

b

Puffins can hold several small fish in their bills at a time because...	the insides of their mouth and tongue are rough and spiny.
	they have long snouts and a tongue that extends up to half a metre.

c

Every year puffins go through their 'annual moult'. This is when...	they shed their skin and grow a whole new set of larger scales.
	they shed their feathers and are unable to fly for a short while.

Task 2   Four of the sentences below are about puffins. Colour the sentences in.

They make very good pets and can live in a bowl of cold water.	They are one of the most popular seabirds, known for being both colourful and full of character.
They are incredibly fast runners and can reach speeds of up to 81 km/h (50 mph).	They are true seabirds and spend most of their time swimming, diving and feeding at sea.
The male is responsible for building the nest and the female lays only one egg in it.	Their sharp claws and strong arms make them expert tree climbers.
They kill their prey by tightly wrapping around it and restricting the flow of blood and oxygen in the animal's body.	Thousands of them nest together in large groups called 'colonies'.

Task 3   Using some of the facts found above, write a short story that tells us a little more about Percy the Puffin.

Percy Puffin lives in a burrow on a high cliff above the cold North Sea. With hundreds of friends and family, Percy _____

_____

_____

_____

_____

Exploring Further ...

Read these titles and predict what the text will be about.

a   **Get crafty: how you can create your own puffin**

_____

_____

b   **Peeking at puffins from past to present**

_____

_____

Now swoop to pages 118–119 to record what you have learned in your Explorer's Logbook.

Understanding what you read

One of the best things about **reading** is that it gives you the ability to **discover** endless **exciting facts** about the world around you. Experts researching animals will often go back to books **written by others** to improve their understanding. On these pages you will use your **comprehension** skills to find out about the rather odd-looking lumpfish!

FACT FILE

Animal:	Lumpfish
Habitat:	Cold waters of the Arctic, North Pacific and North Atlantic
Weight:	Up to 9 kg
Lifespan:	Up to 10 years
Diet:	Small sealife, including shrimp

Task 1

Below is the contents page from a non-fiction book about lumpfish. Which page would you turn to if you wanted to know...

a ... how to identify a lumpfish? ☐

b ... what a word in the book means? ☐

c ... where to find a lumpfish? ☐

d ... if lumpfish are carnivores or not? ☐

e ... how long a lumpfish lives? ☐

Contents

WILD FACT

LUMPFISH get their name from the **LINES OF BONY LUMPS** that cover their **THICK SKIN.**

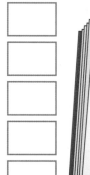
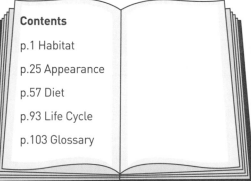

Task 2 Below are some words and four definitions from the glossary of a book. Draw a line to join the correct word to the definition.

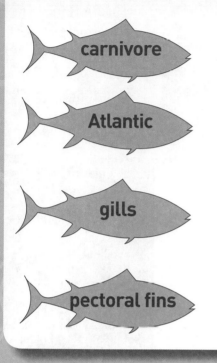

carnivore

Atlantic

gills

pectoral fins

The parts of a fish that allow it to breathe underwater.

The world's second largest ocean, between Europe and Africa to the east, and the Americas to the west.

The parts found either side of a fish's head, used to control movement.

An animal that eats other animals as the key part of its diet.

WILD FACT

LUMPFISH have a **'SUCKING DISC'** on their belly which allows them to **ANCHOR** to **ROCKS** and other objects.

Task 3 Read the non-fiction text below and then write three questions that you think someone should be able to answer from it.

The lumpfish is known by some as the 'lumpsucker'. It has a short, fat body. It does not have scales but rather thick, lumpy skin. Large lumpfish can reach up to 60cm in length and 8 to 9kg in weight. They are found within cold northern waters, such as the North Atlantic. The lumpfish is a carnivore, eating a diet of smaller fish and tiny sea creatures.

1 _____

2 _____

3 _____

Exploring Further …

Show the extract in Task 3 to a friend or family member and ask them your questions. See how well they answer, giving marks out of 3!

1 mark: Try again!

2 marks: Getting saltier . . .

3 marks: Fish and chips for tea!

Now go to pages 118–119 to record what you have learned in your Explorer's Logbook.

Hold the headline!

Headlines are the words in large print at the top of **newspaper** stories. **Tabloid** papers are smaller-sized newspapers that often carry reports about celebrities and sensational stories. **Broadsheet** newspapers carry longer reports and usually have more articles about politics and the economy.

Headlines often use these features to catch people's attention:

- **Alliteration** – using words starting with the same letter, such as:
  PINK PRAWNS PRODUCE PUTRID PONG!

- **Rhyme**, such as:
  FAT CAT MISTAKEN FOR HAT

- Changing a letter or letters to give words a **double meaning**, such as:
  BALDNESS: 'HAIR' TODAY, GONE TOMORROW

- **Puns** – using a word that has two meanings, such as:
  BAKER LOSES A BUN-DLE

WILD FACT

PRAWNS have **TEN PAIRS OF LEGS:** five pairs for swimming and five pairs for walking. Three pairs have **CLAWS** which are used for **FEEDING.**

Task 1   **Match the start of each newspaper report to the headline.**

a Water quality at a coastal resort has improved as a result of action to reduce pollution.

b Residents are being urged to create ponds in their gardens to provide more habitats for local frogs.

c Marine biologists have warned that we need to stop litter and other waste material entering the ocean.

Let's get drastic about plastic

Sea the change!

Jump to it!

Task 2 Are these headlines from a broadsheet newspaper or a tabloid newspaper?

a **King prawn!** – Largest-ever prawn found

_____

b **Fan-shaped tail works wonders** – The science of how prawns steer through water

_____

c **Prawn cocktail!** – Rich variety of prawns were found

_____

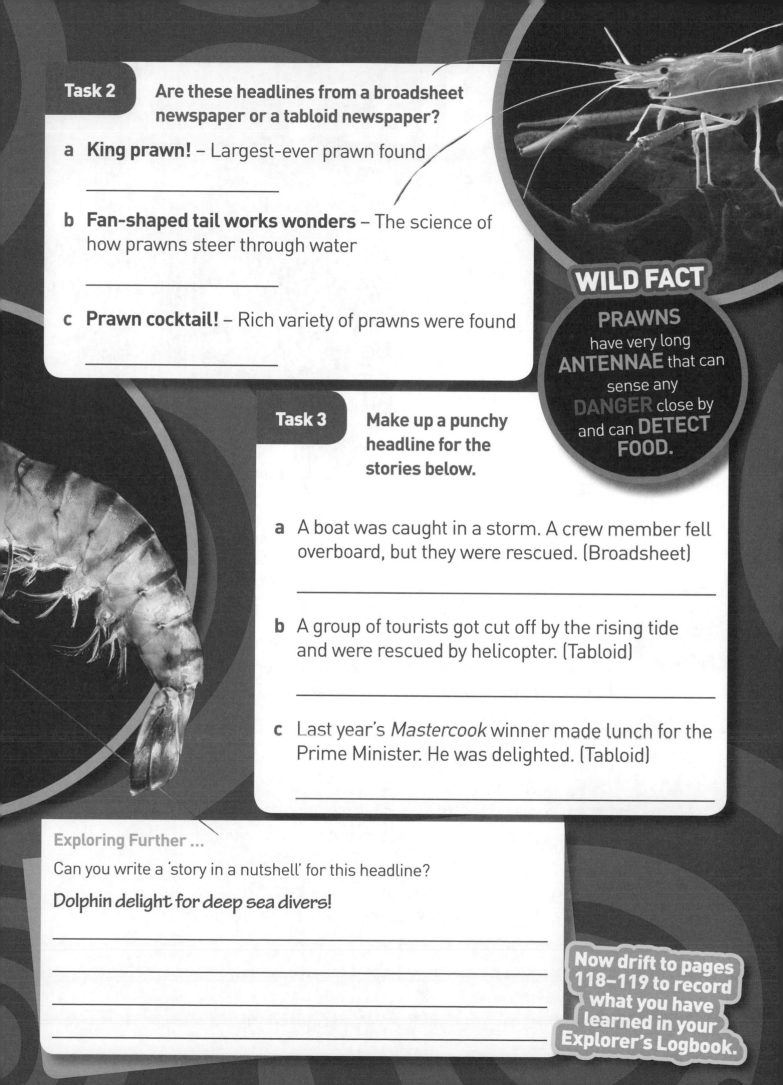

WILD FACT

PRAWNS have very long **ANTENNAE** that can sense any **DANGER** close by and can **DETECT FOOD.**

Task 3 Make up a punchy headline for the stories below.

a A boat was caught in a storm. A crew member fell overboard, but they were rescued. (Broadsheet)

_____

b A group of tourists got cut off by the rising tide and were rescued by helicopter. (Tabloid)

_____

c Last year's *Mastercook* winner made lunch for the Prime Minister. He was delighted. (Tabloid)

_____

Exploring Further ...

Can you write a 'story in a nutshell' for this headline?

Dolphin delight for deep sea divers!

_____
_____
_____
_____

Now drift to pages 118–119 to record what you have learned in your Explorer's Logbook.

Dear diary

A diary is usually written in the **first person**, using 'I' or 'me'. It is written in **chronological** order, with the earliest event first. It is about events that have already happened, so is written in the **past tense**. There should be '**time**' words at the start of some sentences. It will usually contain the thoughts and feelings of the writer, such as:

Today I got up early and went into town. After lunch, we went to the cinema. The film was ace! It was better than the first one, and I loved it!

FACT FiLE

Animal:	Sea otter
Habitat:	The shallow waters of the Pacific Ocean
Weight:	14 to 45 kg
Lifespan:	Up to 23 years
Diet:	Fish and sea urchins

Task 1

Read these diary extracts written by a person watching a sea otter and its cub. Put the events in chronological order by writing a number from 1–5 in the box next to each extract.

a The cub is really starting to get the hang of using its tail to move through the water.

b This afternoon was incredible! A beautiful cub arrived safely into the world. It was born in the water and had its eyes wide open.

c The cub is getting bigger. Soon it'll stop drinking its mother's milk, and it'll be ready to eat some fish.

d The growing cub was able to dive down to get a shell from the sea bed today. It was wonderful to see!

e The newborn cub can't swim far yet, so it usually spends much of the day on its mother's tummy.

Task 2

An online diary is called a 'blog'. Read these extracts from a wildlife photographer's blog about a colony of grey seals and their pups on the UK's Norfolk coast. Put the events in order and draw a line to match each one to the most suitable date.

October 29, 2019

November 10, 2019

November 28, 2019

December 11, 2019

The mums have returned to the sea, leaving the pups on the beach for a bit longer. The pups' white fur is gradually disappearing to leave the dark waterproof coat they will have as adults.

Most of the pups are now in the sea, learning to swim. It's great to see them playing in the waves!

The pups are growing fast! They are putting on a remarkable amount of weight because their mothers' milk is so fattening.

I saw dozens of grey seals caring for their newborn pups on the beach today – it was a wonderful sight!

Task 3

Add some ideas and details to this diary.

WILD FACT

SEA OTTERS have been known to COVER THEMSELVES in KELP SEAWEED to stop themselves from DRIFTING AWAY!

Day 1: I saw the sea otters today. I was excited because _____
_____.

Day 3: One of the younger sea otters was _____ .
I felt _____.

Day 4: It looked like the otters were having a diving competition off the rocks. They were _____ which made me feel _____.

Day 6: One of the otters was cracking open a shell on the rock today. They seem to eat a lot! I wonder _____.

Exploring Further ...

Write a diary entry about a time you have watched wildlife. Use the past tense, start with 'I', and include your thoughts and feelings.

_____
_____
_____

Now find pages 118–119 to record what you have learned in your Explorer's Logbook.

Perfecting your poetry

Poetry is a type of writing that has been around for *thousands* of years. The purpose of a poem is that it gives the author the chance to **express ideas** or **feelings** in a relatively short piece of writing that will interest and entertain the reader.

Many people think that poems have to include rhyming words (like 'bird' and 'heard' or 'white' and 'bright') or have a certain rhythm or pattern when read aloud. This isn't actually true: poems can do anything!

FACT FILE

Animal: Black-headed gull
Habitat: Farmland, wetland and coast in Europe, Asia and Canada
Weight: 200 to 400 g
Lifespan: A maximum recorded lifespan of 32 years!
Diet: Worms, insects and fish

WILD FACT

BLACK-HEADED GULLS often live in LARGE, NOISY GROUPS.

Task 1	For words to rhyme, they must make the same sound when read aloud. Try these – the first one has been done for you.

a gull   rhymes with   *hull*

b black   rhymes with   _____

c fly   rhymes with   _____

d flock   rhymes with   _____

e fish   rhymes with   _____

f eggs   rhymes with   _____

Task 2

Now put each pair of rhyming words into a sentence. The first one is done for you.

a The tired **gull** landed on the ship's **hull**.

b _____.

c _____.

d _____.

e _____.

f _____.

Task 3

Poems are often meant to be told by someone who knows the poem 'off by heart'. Read this poem, then close the book and see if you can still remember it.

<u>The Little Bird</u>

Once I saw a little bird,

Come hop, hop, hop;

So I cried, 'Little bird,

Will you stop, stop, stop?'

And was going to the window,

To say how do you do?

But he shook his little tail,

And far away he flew.

WILD FACT

During summer, the **FEATHERS** on the **GULL'S HEAD** turn a **CHOCOLATE-BROWN** colour.

Exploring Further ...

Now you know the poem of *The Little Bird*, practise saying it out loud, adding expression and ensuring that you add the pauses and breaths where the punctuation shows they should be. When you think you are ready for an audience, try reciting the poem to a friend or your family!

Now land on pages 118–119 to record what you have learned in your Explorer's Logbook.

Explorer's Logbook

Maths: Ages 7–8

Tick off the topics as you complete them and colour in the star to show how you feel.

Addition ☐

Numbers up to 1000 ☐

Mental subtraction ☐

Subtraction ☐

Place value ☐

Mental addition ☐

Multiplication ☐

Money ☐

Multiples ☐

Division ☐

2D shapes ☐

3D shapes ☐

Straight lines ☐

Explorer's Logbook

Maths: Ages 8–9

Tick off the topics as you complete them and colour in the star to show how you feel.

Factors and multiples ☐

Fractions ☐

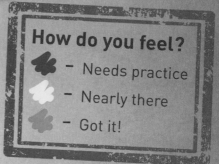

Rounding and negative numbers ☐

Decimals ☐

Number systems ☐

Symmetry ☐

Coordinates & translations ☐

Time ☐

Statistics ☐

Length ☐

Mass ☐

Capacity ☐

Angles ☐

Explorer's Logbook

English: Ages 7–8

Tick off the topics as you complete them and colour in the star to show how you feel.

How do you feel?
- Needs practice
- Nearly there
- Got it!

Apostrophes ☐

Homophones ☐

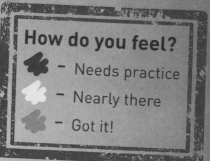

ch words ☐

ou words ☐

y or i? ☐

More apostrophes ☐

Word families ☐

Punctuation ☐

Word endings ☐

le, el, il and al endings ☐

Plurals ☐

Tenses ☐

More tenses ☐

Explorer's Logbook

English: Ages 8–9

Tick off the topics as you complete them and colour in the star to show how you feel.

Delivering details ☐

Syllables ☐

Suffixes ☐

Phonemes ☐

Punctuation ☐

Prefixes ☐

How do you know? ☐

Perfecting your poetry ☐

Understanding what you read ☐

Dear diary ☐

Conjunctions ☐

Hold the headline! ☐

What happens next? ☐

Answers Maths Ages 7–8

Pages 8–9

Task 1

a 2 ones = 2
b 5 hundreds = 500
c 9 tens = 90
d 6 ones = 6
e 5 tens = 50
f 3 hundreds = 300

Task 2

a 56
b 27
c 628
d 304

Task 3

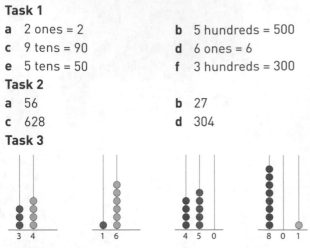

Exploring Further...

	Hundreds	Tens	Ones	
150		1	6	166
540		5	7	597
610		7	1	681
320	4	4	3	763
430	2	2	8	658

Pages 10–11

Task 1

a forty-three
b ninety-one
c two hundred and fifty-eight
d seven hundred and seven

Task 2

a 77
b 618
c 999

Task 3

a 545 540 504 454 450 405
b 11 101 110 111 121 211

Task 4

a 169 170 171 172 173 174
b 581 591 601 611 621 631

Exploring Further...

a 873
b 378
c 783

Pages 12–13

Task 1

a 858
b 680
c 963
d 313
e 231
f 719
g 907
h 370

Task 2

a 482
b 196
c 300
d 444
e 662
f 559
g 384
h 842

Task 3

a 881
b 901
c 936
d 903

Exploring Further...

208	965	160	17	395	58	471	178	36	47	729	28	653
909	398	492	56	824	25	57	93	97	798	74	30	67
27	48	86	593	92	77	54	149	91	207	772	229	41
643	81	741	19	62	482	87	150	903	712	797	845	78
45	68	88	663	303	999	697	6	85	505	228	99	37

Pages 14–15

Task 1

a 761
b 807
c 714
d 929
e 762
f 511
g 392
h 283

Task 2

a 195
b 312
c 350
d 301

Task 3

a 608
b 65
c 44

Exploring Further...

a 83 and 62, 33 and 54
b 37
c 33
d 54

Pages 16–17

Task 1

a 85
b 179
c 89
d 101

Task 2

a 965
b 329
c 310
d 605

Task 3

491

Exploring Further...

a 364 + 47 + 258 = 669
b 497 + 306 + 83 = 886
c 59 + 327 + 109 = 495

Pages 18–19

Task 1

a 806
b 912

Task 2

a 27
b 45
c 32
d 331

Task 3

a 285
b 570
c 211
d 39

Exploring Further...

a 27 cm
b 48 cm

Pages 20–21

Task 1

a 18, 20, **22**, **24**, 26, 28, **30**, **32**
b 18, **21**, **24**, 27, 30, **33**, 36, **39**
c **16**, 20, **24**, 28, 32, **36**, 40, **44**
d 15, 20, **25**, **30**, **35**, 40, 45, **50**

Task 2

a 20, 60, 30, 100
b 24, 48, 80, 96
c 8, 48, 32
d 12, 30
e 50, 60, 10
f 100, 200, 600

Task 3

a 30
b 72

Exploring Further...

Tadpole 1 becomes Frog C

Tadpole 2 becomes Frog A

Tadpole 3 becomes Frog B

Pages 22–23

Task 1

a i 6   ii 15   iii 12   iv 18

b i 18   ii 20   iii 16   iv 22

c i 28   ii 40   iii 56   iv 24

Task 2

a 32 + 640 = 672   b 10 + 140 = 150

Task 3

a 445   b 296   c 184   d 282

Task 4

a 480   b 320   c 350   d 200

Exploring Further...

a 7 cm × 4 = 28 cm   b 6 cm × 5 = 30 cm

c 4 × 5 = 20

Pages 24–25

Task 1

a i 12   ii 6   iii 10   iv 9

b i 6   ii 8   iii 3   iv 12

c i 7   ii 8   iii 7   iv 8

d i 9   ii 6   iii 4   iv 7

Task 2

a 20   b 30   c 30   d 60

e 100   f 200   g 20   h 175

Task 3

a 34   b 31   c 42

d 20   e 23   f 13

Exploring Further...

Sandwiches 4   Apples 2

Grapes 8   Packet of crisps $\frac{1}{2}$

Biscuits 1

Pages 26–27

Task 1

a 77p   b 47p

c £1.05   d £5.42

Task 2

a Spent 71p   29p change

b Spent 80p   20p change

c Spent £1.76   24p change

d Spent £1.92   8p change

e Spent £2.52   £2.48 change

Exploring Further...

a Scott £3   b Scott

   Ismail £4.40

   Beth £3

   Daisy £3.50

Pages 28–29

Task 1

a horizontal   b diagonal   c horizontal

d vertical   e diagonal

Task 2

a and d ticked

Task 3

b and d ticked

Exploring Further...

a   i   ii

or any other suitable answers

b horizontal   c vertical

Pages 30–31

Task 1

a

b

or any other suitable answers

Task 2

Quadrilateral	Not a quadrilateral
C, F, G, H, J, K	A, B, D, E, I, L, M

Task 3

No right angles	1 right angle	2 right angles	4 right angles
A, B, G, H, I, J, M	E, L	D, K	C, F

Exploring Further...

	Some equal sides	No equal sides
One or more right angles	C, F	D, E, K, L
No right angles	A, B, G, H, I, J	M

Pages 32–33

Task 1

ice cream cone: cone   football: sphere

cereal packet: cuboid   toilet roll: cylinder

Task 2

a hexagon   b pentagon

c rectangle / square   d square

Task 3

Shape	Faces	Edges	Vertices
Square-based pyramid	5	8	5
Cylinder	3	2	0
Pentagonal prism	7	15	10
Hexagonal prism	8	18	12

Exploring Further...

a 7 faces   b 15 edges   c 10 vertices

Answers Maths Ages 8–9

Pages 34–35

Task 1
a 50   **b** 920   **c** 6810   **d** 4050   **e** 7900
f 6   **g** 26   **h** 548   **i** 301   **j** 950

Task 2
a 400   **b** 6900   **c** 2900   **d** 3600
e 40   **f** 35   **g** 71   **h** 24

Task 3
a 15   **b** 24   **c** 61   **d** 90
e XVI   **f** XXXV   **g** LII   **h** XXVI

Exploring Further...
a ×10   **b** ÷10   **c** ÷100   **d** ÷10   **e** ×100

Pages 36–37

Task 1
a 20   **b** 80   **c** 40   **d** 710   **e** 260   **f** 500

Task 2
a 500   **b** 800   **c** 400   **d** 2800   **e** 7500   **f** 9000

Task 3
a 4000   **b** 4000   **c** 8000

Task 4
a −4, −3, −2, −1, 0, 1, 2, 3
b −8, −6, −4, −2, 0, 2, 4, 6
c −12, −8, −4, 0, 4, 8, 12, 16
d −16, −11, −6, −1, 4, 9, 14, 19
e −8, −5, −2, 1, 4, 7, 10, 13

Exploring Further...

	Round to the nearest ten	Round to the nearest hundred	Round to the nearest thousand
3117	3120	3100	3000
5351	5350	5400	5000
2459	2460	2500	2000
4965	4970	5000	5000
4293	4290	4300	4000
3969	3970	4000	4000

Pages 38–39

Task 1
1 and 30, 2 and 15, 3 and 10, 5 and 6

Task 2
a 5   **b** 4   **c** 8   **d** 3

Task 3
a 36, 12, 18, 30   **b** 35, 42, 28, 84
c 81, 27, 72, 63   **d** 50, 525, 775

Task 4
a 2000   3000   4000   5000   6000   7000
b 16   24   32   40   48   56
c 14   21   28   35   42   49
d 18   27   36   45   54   63

Exploring Further...
a 48

1	2	3	4	6	8	12	16	24	48

45

1	3	5	9	15	45

42

1	2	3	6	7	14	21	42

b 1 and 3
c 1, 2, 3 and 6

Pages 40–41

Task 1
a i $\frac{1}{5} = \frac{2}{10}$ ii $\frac{4}{5} = \frac{8}{10}$ iii 2
b i $\frac{1}{4} = \frac{2}{8}$ ii $\frac{3}{4} = \frac{6}{8}$ iii 2
c i $\frac{1}{10} = \frac{10}{100}$ ii $\frac{7}{10} = \frac{70}{100}$ iii 10

Task 2
a i $\frac{4}{10} = \frac{2}{5}$ ii $\frac{6}{10} = \frac{3}{5}$ iii 2
b i $\frac{4}{8} = \frac{2}{4}$ ii $\frac{6}{8} = \frac{3}{4}$ iii 2
c i $\frac{30}{100} = \frac{3}{10}$ ii $\frac{50}{100} = \frac{5}{10}$ iii 10

Task 3
a $\frac{6}{9} = \frac{2}{3}$ **b** $\frac{4}{8} = \frac{1}{2}$ **c** $\frac{9}{12} = \frac{3}{4}$ **d** $\frac{6}{10} = \frac{3}{5}$

Exploring Further...
$\frac{3}{4} = \frac{6}{8}$ $\frac{1}{6} = \frac{12}{72}$ $\frac{2}{5} = \frac{4}{10}$ $\frac{5}{8} = \frac{15}{24}$ $\frac{1}{2} = \frac{9}{18}$ $\frac{3}{7} = \frac{9}{21}$

$\frac{2}{3} = \frac{8}{12}$ $\frac{7}{10} = \frac{14}{20}$

Pages 42–43

Task 1
a 0.3   **b** 0.7   **c** 0.45   **d** 0.36   **e** 0.5
f $\frac{9}{10}$ **g** $\frac{1}{10}$ **h** $\frac{6}{10}$ **i** $\frac{87}{100}$ **j** $\frac{25}{100}$

Task 2
a 34   **b** 59   **c** 73.1   **d** 40.2   **e** 6.1   **f** 8.2   **g** 2.57   **h** 0.13
i 264   **j** 492   **k** 830   **l** 20   **m** 3.49   **n** 6.81   **o** 0.56   **p** 0.43

Task 3
a 6 tenths, $\frac{6}{10}$ **b** 4 tenths, $\frac{4}{10}$
c 1 hundredth, $\frac{1}{100}$ **d** 3 hundredths, $\frac{3}{100}$

Task 4
a 4   **b** 6   **c** 2   **d** 46

Exploring Further...

	0.8	$\frac{8}{10}$	$\frac{80}{100}$	$\frac{4}{5}$	0.80
a	0.5	$\frac{1}{2}$	0.50	$\frac{5}{10}$	$\frac{50}{100}$
b	0.1	$\frac{10}{100}$	0.10	$\frac{1}{10}$	
c	0.25	$\frac{1}{4}$	$\frac{25}{100}$		
d	0.75	$\frac{3}{4}$	$\frac{75}{100}$		
e	0.7	$\frac{7}{10}$	0.70	$\frac{70}{100}$	

Pond skater **a** gets the furthest.

Pages 44–45

Task 1
a $\frac{1}{10}$ cm = 0.1 cm   **b** $\frac{7}{10}$ cm = 0.7 cm
c $\frac{9}{10}$ cm = 0.9 cm   **d** $2\frac{1}{10}$ cm = 2.1 cm

Task 2
a $\frac{43}{100}$ m = 0.43 m   **b** $\frac{57}{100}$ m = 0.57 m
c $\frac{21}{100}$ m = 0.21 m   **d** $1\frac{89}{100}$ m = 1.89 m

Task 3
a 2(5 + 4) cm = 18 cm   **b** 2(6 + 2) cm = 16 cm
c 2(3 + 3) m = 12 m

Task 4
a 8 squares   **b** $8\frac{1}{2}$ squares

Exploring Further...

	First habitat	Second habitat	Difference in mm	Difference in cm
Centipede	15 mm	2 cm	5 mm	0.5 cm
Woodlouse	25 mm	2.7 cm	2 mm	0.2 cm
Earthworm	85 mm	7 cm	15 mm	1.5 cm
Millipede	19 mm	2.5 cm	6 mm	0.6 cm
Grasshopper	57 mm	4.3 cm	14 mm	1.4 cm

Pages 46–47

Task 1
Elephant: 3 tonnes; Dog: 13 kilograms; Aphid: 0.2 milligrams

Task 2
a 2 kg 731 g **b** 5 kg 802 g **c** 6 kg 91 g **d** 4 kg 400 g
e 9 t 263 kg **f** 4 t 905 kg **g** 8 t 12 kg **h** 3 t 200 kg

Task 3
a 5500 g **b** 8086 g **c** 4009 g **d** 2349 g

Task 4
a 8274 mg **b** 3700 mg **c** 5024 mg **d** 7002 mg

Task 5
a 7201 kg, 7 t 70 kg, 721 kg, 7210 g, 7 kg 2 g, 721 g
b 4003 g, 3 kg 54 g, 3045 g, 4035 mg, 4 g 5 mg, 4 g

Exploring Further...
a
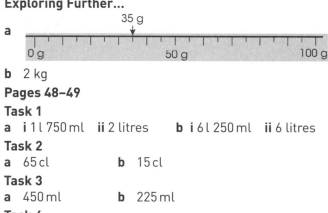
35 g

0 g   50 g   100 g

b 2 kg

Pages 48–49

Task 1
a i 1 l 750 ml **ii** 2 litres **b i** 6 l 250 ml **ii** 6 litres

Task 2
a 65 cl **b** 15 cl

Task 3
a 450 ml **b** 225 ml

Task 4
a 75 ml, 75 cl, 755 ml, 7.5 l, 7505 ml, 7500 cl
b 47 ml, 410 ml, 4 l, 4001 ml, 401 cl, 4.1 l

Exploring Further...
1500 ml and 50 cl, 1.2 l and 80 cl, 1 l and 100 cl,
60 cl and 1400 ml, 200 ml and 1800 ml

Pages 50–51

Task 1
5 past 6 in the morning	06:05
quarter to 9 in the evening	20:45
quarter past 3 in the afternoon	15:15
25 minutes to 2 in the afternoon	13:35
6 minutes to 8 in the morning	07:54

Task 2
a 23:43 **b** 11:21 **c** 08:13 **d** 18:57 **e** 13:25

Task 3
Paula, Philip and Patricia are all correct.

Task 4
a 420 minutes **b** 1800 seconds **c** 108 months **d** 56 days

Exploring Further...
a 12 **b** 8 **c** 4

Pages 52–53

Task 1
a acute **b** acute **c** obtuse **d** right angle

Task 2
a acute **b** obtuse **c** obtuse
d right angle **e** acute **f** acute

Task 3
f, b, c, d, a, e

Exploring Further...
a unequal **b** unequal **c** equal **d** equal

Pages 54–55

Task 1
a Yes **b** Yes **c** No **d** No

Task 2
b and **c** ticked

Task 3
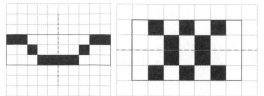

Exploring Further...

Pages 56–57

Task 1
a (3, 1) **b** (1, 6) **c** (10, 4) **d** (5, 8)

Task 2
3 squares right, 2 squares up

Task 3

Exploring Further...

Point D is (8, 2).

Pages 58–59

Task 1
a ant **b** centipede **c** 15 **d** 37

Task 2
a August **b** 10 **c** October **d** September

Exploring Further...
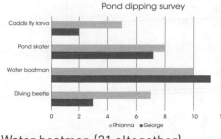
Pond dipping survey

Water boatman (21 altogether)

Answers English Ages 7-8

Pages 60–61

Task 1

a their **b** one **c** hear **d** too **e** hair **f** tails

Task 2

a dew **b** grown **c** sun **d** grate **e** pear or pare **f** bare

Task 3

Any sentence is acceptable that is grammatically correct and uses the given word in an appropriate context.

Exploring Further...

a real, reel   **b** floor, flaw   **c** right, write

d blue, blew   **e** bean, been

Pages 62–63

Task 1

unsafe, safety, safest

reapply, apply, application

familiarity, unfamiliar, familiarise

Task 2

Possible answers include:

a container, contained, containing

b regrettable, regretful

c allowed, allowance, allowable

d following, follower, followed

Task 3

a football player   **b** school playground

c playful puppy   **d** playing tennis

Exploring Further...

V	A	L	A	V	U	E	D	L
D	L	L	E	A	L	N	F	D
B	E	V	A	L	U	A	T	E
S	U	A	S	U	V	A	E	U
V	A	L	U	A	B	L	E	L
T	T	U	W	T	B	I	D	A
L	U	E	E	I	C	L	M	V
O	E	R	T	O	T	I	E	L
Y	D	L	M	N	L	L	V	E

Pages 64–65

Task 1

a chair, chill, charm   **b** monarch, mechanic, echo

c chalet, chandelier, brochure

Task 2

a stomach **b** shampoo **c** chaos

d technical **e** machine **f** chivalry

Task 3

Any sentences are acceptable which are grammatically correct and use the given word in an appropriate context.

Exploring Further...

a anchor **b** moustache **c** chain **d** parachute

Pages 66–67

Task 1

a mystery **b** history **c** rhythm

d riddle **e** habit **f** prettily

Task 2

a myth **b** symbol **c** wriggle

d optimist **e** typical **f** critical

Task 3

a cymbals – round metal musical instrument

b anonymous – of unknown name

c syrup – thick, sticky sugary liquid

d syllable – beats in a word

e platypus – Australian animal

Exploring Further...

E	D	N	O	E	L	E	A
D	K	L	O	G	A	M	P
S	O	N	E	I	P	C	H
S	Y	M	P	H	O	N	Y
X	L	S	K	O	A	L	S
O	N	Y	T	X	D	J	I
W	O	P	S	E	N	Q	C
A	L	Y	D	I	M	Y	A
A	M	L	E	A	Y	A	U

Pages 68–69

Task 1

a discourage **b** nourish **c** burrow **d** bunting

e tough   **f** wrung   **g** hung   **h** spurt

Task 2

a currage – courage   **b** cupple – couple

c flurrish – flourish   **d** trubble – trouble

e rugh – rough

Task 3

a touch **b** double **c** young **d** rough

Task 4

a jealous   **b** famous   **c** hazardous

d fabulous   **e** nervous   **f** various

g obvious   **h** curious

Exploring Further...

Any sentence is acceptable which is grammatically correct and uses the given words in an appropriate context.

Pages 70–71

Task 1

a explorer's **b** sun's **c** scientists' **d** horses'

e ladies'   **f** mare's **g** pony's **h** children's

Task 2

Singular	Plural
horse's ear	horses' ears
man's hat	men's hats
child's toy	children's toys
baby's rattle	babies' rattles
woman's book	women's books
person's vote	people's votes
animal's foot	animals' feet

Task 3

a No People's   **b** No Falabella's

c No book's   **d** No horse's

e Yes trainer's

Exploring Further...

a TRUE   **b** FALSE   **c** TRUE

Pages 72–73

Task 1
a do not – don't **b** she is – she's
c we are – we're **d** he will – he'll
e I am – I'm **f** we will not – we won't

Task 2
a shouldn't **b** they're **c** won't **d** aren't **e** we'd **f** you're

Task 3
a she'll: w i **b** they'd: w o u l **or** h a
c can't: n o **d** it's: i **or** h a
e they're: a **f** it'll: w i

Exploring Further...
Across: **2.** it would **3.** could not **4.** I have **5.** we have
Down: **1.** should have

Pages 74–75

Task 1
a mansion **b** passion **c** optician
d electrician **e** pension **f** permission

Task 2
a mission **b** confession **c** tension
d musician **e** politician **f** extension

Task 3
Any sentence is acceptable which is grammatically correct and uses the given word in an appropriate context.

Exploring Further...
a INVENTION **b** ADMISSION **c** RATION

Pages 76–77

Task 1
a A pygmy marmoset is about 15 cm long.
b Have you ever seen a pygmy marmoset?
c Those monkeys are totally amazing!
d Have you discovered where marmosets live?
e A pygmy marmoset is the world's smallest monkey.

Task 2
a The pygmy marmoset feasted on sap, leaves and berries.
b The explorer packed water, food, a map and a compass for the journey.
c You find out about wildlife from zoos, libraries and websites.
d Pygmy marmosets are found in Brazil, Peru, Colombia and Ecuador.
e The pygmy marmoset is prey for cats, eagles, hawks and snakes.

Task 3
a 'There's a marmoset in that tree!' exclaimed the explorer.
b 'I managed to take a photograph of it,' replied the wildlife photographer.
c The explorer commented, 'That will look great in our logbook.'
d 'I'll see if I can take another one,' added the photographer.
e 'I can count nine marmosets in that tree!' said Akemi.

Exploring Further...
The explorers trekked into the forest. They saw colourful birds, tiny frogs and large snakes.
'Look up there!' shouted their guide. 'Can you see the marmosets in the trees?'

Pages 78–79

Task 1
walk – walked search – searched
bring – brought wake – woke
live – lived sleep – slept

Task 2
a found **b** was **c** took **d** let

Task 3
a The explorers are finding out about the wildlife on Barbados.
b I am hoping they are able to find the tiny eggs of the Barbados threadsnake.
c Scientists are discovering more about them every day.

Exploring Further...
a past **b** future **c** present

Pages 80–81

Task 1
a table **b** metal **c** label
d fossil **e** rebel **f** stable

Task 2
a squirrel **b** capital **c** nostril
d towel **e** bottle **f** nibble

Task 3
a traval – travel **b** animel – animal
c middel – middle **d** littal – little
e cradel – cradle

Exploring Further...
Across: **1.** pencil **2.** medal **3.** table
Down: **4.** camel **5.** apple

Pages 82–83

Task 1
a have studied **b** have fallen
c have cared for **d** has found
e have seen

Task 2
c

Task 3
a has laid **b** has looked
c have protected

Exploring Further...

W	L	A	E	K	W
A	R	A	N	J	E
S	S	O	A	E	K
L	E	A	T	L	O
R	K	K	N	E	W
U	N	E	C	F	K
N	E	S	W	T	Q

Pages 84–85

Task 1
a explorers **b** foxes **c** wishes
d pebbles **e** ladies **f** monkeys

Task 2
a shelves **b** ponies **c** deer
d men **e** lives **f** feet

Task 3

Add s	Add es	Remove the y and add ies	Remove the f and add ves
forest	witch	poppy	loaf
creature	bus	party	leaf
key	glass	discovery	half

Exploring Further...
a CHILDREN – child **b** TEETH – tooth
c PEOPLE – person **d** GEESE – goose
e LICE – louse

Answers English Ages 8-9

Pages 86–87

Task 1
a 1 **b** 3 **c** 2 **d** 2 **e** 4 **f** 2 **g** 1 **h** 3 **i** 2 **j** 5

Task 2
a pi-a-no **b** his-tory **c** cal-en-dar **d** ex-per-i-ment

Task 3
a heart **b** famous **c** busy **d** remember

Exploring Further...

Monosyllabic words	Disyllabic words	Polysyllabic words
shark	turtle puffin dolphin	camera jellyfish crocodile (or 'alligator')

Pages 88–89

Task 1
a ca**tch** **b** cli**mb** **c** **kn**it **d** **wr**ong **e** **n**ear **f** pin**ch**
g **ch**emist **h** **ph**one **i** **kn**owledge **j** le**dge**

Task 2

fr**oot**	fruit	w**ate**	wait / weight
g**ide**	guide	wr**oat**	wrote
br**yt**	bright	compl**eat**	complete
gr**oop**	group	br**iethe**	breathe
b**ede**	bead	extr**eam**	extreme

Task 3
a school **b** hei**gh**t **c** peng**u**in **d** swallow **e** sea

Exploring Further...

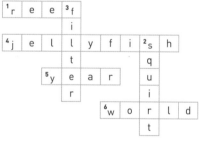

Pages 90–91

Task 1

in-	im-	ir-	il-
indescribable invalid	immature impersonal improbable	irreplaceable irregular irrational	illogical illiterate

Task 2
Use **il** for words that begin with 'l'.
Use **ir** for words that begin with 'r'.
Use **im** for words that begin with 'm' or 'p'.
Use **in** for words that begin with all other letters.

Task 3

Root word	Add correct prefix
legal	il
correct, visible, formal, expensive	in
responsible	ir
possible	im

Exploring Further...

in	active	im	legible	in	correct
il	migrant	possible	ir	polite	il
formal	in	il	legal	im	right
ir	im	expensive	ir	luminate	in
patient	correct	im	regular	il	relevant
responsible	il	in	patient	adequate	im

Pages 92–93

Task 1
a victorious **b** nervous **c** dangerous
d glorious **e** courageous **f** poisonous

Task 2
a cautious **b** venomous **c** famous
d mountainous **e** various

Task 3
Remove the final vowel and add the **ous** suffix.

Exploring Further...
ambitious, infectious, hazardous, mysterious

Pages 94–95

Task 1
(bird) (fish) (crab) (man) ~~deadly~~ ~~poisonous~~ ~~smooth~~
crawl swim sleep swoop ~~patterned~~

Task 2
Gently, → I go swimming.
Once a week, → he leapt forward.
Suddenly, → I love to read.
On holiday, → he lifted up the baby.

Task 3
For example: The spiny dogfish migrated south, etc.

Exploring Further...
For example: Unexpectedly, the small, spotty dogfish shot out from behind the large, limpet-covered rock where it had been hiding to avoid being seen.

Pages 96–97

Task 1
a The bright colours of the sea slug are simply amazing!
b Do sea slugs live on coral?
c Remarkably, there are over 1000 species of sea slug!
d How does a sea slug eat?
e How many species of sea slug are there?

Task 2
(It's), don't, they're, aren't, can't, I've

Task 3
a **M**ore than 500 species of sea slug live on **A**ustralia's **G**reat **B**arrier **R**eef**.**
b **D**idn't you know that sea slugs can regenerate parts of their body**?**
c **"B**rilliant! **I've** seen a sea slug**,"** thought the scuba diver**.**

Exploring Further...
Did you win?

Pages 98–99

Task 1
a and **b** but **c** because (**or** since) **d** since (**or** because) **e** so

Task 2

Brittle stars can be found in ~~sees~~ all over the world. They have teeny bodies and five long arms with spiky bits on them. Brittle stars can break off these arms to escape meat-eating animals that hunt them. The arms quickly grow back in some species. Brittle stars can move fast in any direction ~~usin~~ ~~there~~ arms like legs. Some people call them serpent stars ~~coz~~ they think they move like snakes. They are hard to spot as they ~~manely~~ come out at night.

Task 3

a   teeny – small
b   animals that hunt – predators
c   grow back – regenerate
d   meat-eating – carnivorous
e   come out at night – nocturnal

Exploring Further...

Writing to link ideas in a sensible, free-flowing way, with correct spellings and sentences correctly punctuated.

Pages 100–101

Task 1

upset   surprised   happy   worried   grumpy

Task 2

a   "I really <u>wanted</u> to go to the beach today," said the boy with a <u>glum</u> face. "But can we go <u>tomorrow</u> instead?"
Disappointed *or* sad, hopeful
b   The children <u>crept</u> towards a rockpool and <u>cautiously</u> looked over the edge. The bottom wasn't visible from the surface. "Are you sure we need to find it?" asked the girl.
Worried, anxious *or* nervous
c   The little boy <u>raced</u> across the beach, his bucket swinging wildly. Suddenly, he stopped, and then poked a large pebble with his toe. <u>"Got one, Dad!" he yelled.</u> Excited, delighted

Task 3

a   The woman is pleased, relieved.
b   The woman is worried, alarmed or upset.

Exploring Further...

Your own picture with a speech bubble.

Pages 102–103

Task 1

a   The puffin's bright... → 'the sea parrot'...
b   Puffins can hold... → the insides of their mouth...
c   Every year puffins... → they shed their feathers...

Task 2

Thousands of them nest together in large groups called 'colonies'.	They are one of the most popular seabirds, known for being both colourful and full of character.
The male is responsible for building the nest and the female lays only one egg in it.	They are true seabirds and spend most of their time swimming, diving and feeding at sea.

Task 3

Any correctly spelt story.

Exploring Further...

Any sensible answers, e.g.
a   Instructions for making a model puffin
b   A bird-watcher's memories of observing puffins

Pages 104–105

Task 1

a Page 25   b Page 103   c Page 1   d Page 57   e Page 93

Task 2

carnivore An animal that eats ...
Atlantic The world's second ...
gills The parts of fish that allow it to breathe...
pectoral fins The parts found either side of a fish's head...

Task 3

For example:
By what name is the lumpfish also known as?
The lumpfish is not covered in scales. What is it covered in?
Which ocean are lumpfish found in?
How big are fully grown lumpfish?
What do lumpfish eat?

Exploring Further...

Ask your family or a friend the questions in Task 3.

Pages 106–107

Task 1

a   Sea the change!   b   Jump to it!
c   Let's get drastic about plastic

Task 2

a   Tabloid   b   Broadsheet   c   Tabloid

Task 3

For example:
a   Man in deep water now safe
b   Dramatic air rescue for trapped tourists
c   Exquisite eats for PM

Exploring Further...

Any happy story involving dolphins and deep sea divers.

Pages 108–109

Task 1

a 4   b 1   c 3   d 5   e 2

Task 2

October 29, 2019	I saw dozens of grey seals caring for their newborn pups on the beach today – it was a wonderful sight!
November 10, 2019	The pups are growing fast! They are putting on a remarkable amount of weight because their mothers' milk is so fattening.
November 28, 2019	The mums have returned to the sea, leaving the pups on the beach for a bit longer. The pups' white fur is gradually disappearing to leave the dark waterproof coat they will have as adults.
December 11, 2019	Most of the pups are now in the sea, learning to swim. It's great to see them playing in the waves!

Task 3

Any answer that makes sense and adds detail.

Exploring Further...

A diary entry about wildlife that includes the stated features.

Pages 110–111

Task 1

For example:
b   clack, sack, crack, flack, stack
c   try, my, cry, buy, die, sigh
d   lock, stock, mock, clock, sock
e   dish, wish, swish
f   legs, begs, pegs, kegs

Task 2

Depends on the words chosen in Task 1. For example:
b   There are stacks of black sacks.
c   Don't cry – it's only a fly!
d   The flock played with a dirty sock.
e   How I wish for a fish!
f   Move your legs and collect the eggs!

Task 3

Learn the poem.

Exploring Further...

Recite the poem from memory.

You're awesome!

Well done, you have finished your adventures!

Explorer's pass

Name:_____

Age: _____

Date: _____

Draw a picture of yourself in the box!